Sam Hawkins
Celebrates Cross Stitch

Sam Hawkins
Celebrates Cross Stitch

David & Charles

A DAVID & CHARLES BOOK

First published in the UK in 2000
Designs Copyright © Sam Hawkins 2000
Photography, text and layout Copyright © David & Charles 2000

A catalogue record for this book is available from the British Library.

ISBN 0 7153 1015 1

Photography by John Gollop
Styling by Susan Penny
Designed and produced by Penny & Penny
Printed in Italy by Lego
for David & Charles
Brunel House   Newton Abbot   Devon

Contents

⟨∧⟩ ⟨Y⟩ ⟨⊥⟩ ⟨↘⟩ ⟨●⟩ ⟨↙⟩ ⟨◆⟩ ⟨+⟩ ⟨C⟩ ⟨↑⟩

Introduction

We all like to celebrate important events in our lives and the lives of those around us. Whether it is the arrival of a new baby, a family wedding or a child's birthday there can be no nicer way to commemorate the day than with a hand-stitched gift.

The designs in this book are split into five chapters each covering a range of celebrations in life's colourful tapestry, and each opening with a large sampler or picture. For Baby's Arrival a birth sampler; Home Sweet Home a sampler of peace and love; Childhood Days a fairy-tale sampler; Family & Friends a teddy sampler; and for Romantic moments a portrait of lovers meeting in a woodland glade. The designs featured in 'Celebrates' are presented in new and exciting ways on projects as large as a baby quilt to quick-to-stitch designs for cards and gifts. Whatever the size of the project each comes with detailed stitching and making up instructions, so that whether you are new to cross stitch or a seasoned professional you are sure to find a design that you will enjoy stitching. At the end of each chapter you will find a design collection, a library of projects that will take you through most of the stitching occasions in life.

Cross stitch is a very pleasurable pastime, surrounded by a sea of coloured threads you will feel relaxed, and be taken away from the stresses and strains of modern day living, and into a world of beauty and creativity. With over 100 designs to choose from, we are sure this book will bring you hours of joy both in the stitching and in the giving.

Baby's Arrival

Of all the celebrations in life, a baby's birth is an occasion that welcomes a hand stitched gift. The beautiful designs in this chapter are in soft colours and feature cute animals and fun images just right for a new born baby. The toy box birth sampler with a teddy and jack-in-the-box design can be personalised adding baby's name and date of birth; or for a more practical gift stitch the hooded baby towel, feeding cup or bootees. The animal designs used for the quilt are stitched on Zweigart lincoln fabric, worked over two threads. Brightly coloured cotton gingham has been used to piece the quilt together, which is lined with cotton batting, making the quilt soft, warm and machine washable. The quilt is sure to be loved by the new baby and then passed down through the generations to become a family heirloom

This fun sampler would make a wonderful addition to any nursery wall. The bootees are stitched using the clown chart on page 22.

Toy Box Sampler

To personalise the toy box sampler use the alphabet and numbers chart on pages 118-121 to add baby's name and date of birth

- *White Aida fabric, 14 count 35x42.5cm (14x17in)*
- *DMC stranded cotton (floss) in the colours listed in the key*
- *Tapestry needle, No 24*
- *Picture frame and mount of your choice*

1 Mark the centre of your Aida fabric with tacking stitches and oversew the edges to prevent fraying. Mount the fabric in a frame or embroidery hoop.

2 Work the design from the centre out following the chart and key on pages 18 and 19. Use two strands of stranded cotton (floss) for the cross stitch and one strand for the backstitch and french knots.

3 Personalise the sampler with baby's name and birth date using two strands of stranded cotton (floss) for the cross stitch and the backstitch, and following the chart on pages 118-121. Use graph paper to plan the lettering, and then count the starting position on the fabric before you begin stitching.

Framing the sampler

1 Wash and press your stitching following the instructions on page 124. Take your work to a framer for mounting and framing, or frame it yourself following the instructions on page 124.

Teddy's mouth has been backstitched using black stranded cotton (floss), and then his eyes and nose highlighted with french knots worked in white.

Baby Quilt

To make the quilt fully washable use cotton fabric for all the layers. Quilt around each panel with large running stitches, which will hold the layers firmly together while the quilt is in use

- *White Zweigart lincoln fabric, 14 count 153x25.5cm (60x10in)*
- *DMC stranded cotton (floss) in the colours listed in the key*
- *Cotton gingham fabric –*
  A mauve, two x 10x51cm (4x20¼in)
  B blue, three x 11x22cm (4¼x8¼in)
  C mauve, two x 13x51cm (5¼x20¼in)
  D mauve, two x 12x78cm (4¾x31in)
  E pink, four x 6.25x100cm (2½x39½in)
  F blue, four x 12x13cm (4¾x5¼in)
  G mauve, one x 71x100cm (28x39½in)
- *Warm and Natural 100% cotton needled batting 71x100cm (28x39½in)*
- *Tapestry needle, No 24*
- *White sewing thread and needle*
- *White tacking thread*

1 Cut the lincoln fabric into six 25.5cm (10in) squares. Mark the centre of each square with tacking stitches and oversew around the fabric edges to prevent fraying. Mount each piece in a frame or embroidery hoop.

2 Work each design from the centre out following the charts and keys on pages 20 and 21. The border edge is added around each of the central panels following the horse chart on page 20 for position. The border hearts are worked in the same colour for all the designs, but the double row of backstitch around the edge changes colour for each design: mauve 208 for the duck; orange 351 for the rabbit; blue 518 for the bear; green 470 for the

horse; yellow 743 for the lamb; pink 3731 for the zebra. Use three strands of stranded cotton (floss) for the cross stitch, two strands for the backstitch, and two strands for the french knots, working each stitch over two threads of fabric. Cut the finished cross stitched squares down to 22cm (8¾in). Oversew the edges to prevent fraying.

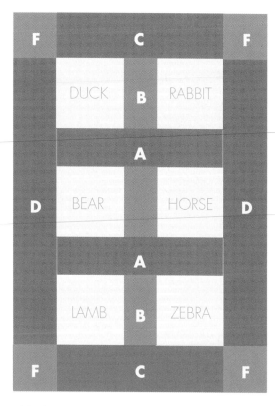

Assemble the quilt top in strips going across the fabric, then add the sides and finally the top panels. Batting is then sandwiched between the top and the backing layer and the layers are held together with large running stitches. The quilt is finished with a binding strip.

Use the diagram on the left as a guide for the tacking stitches; and the diagram on the right to quilt the layers together using running stitches.

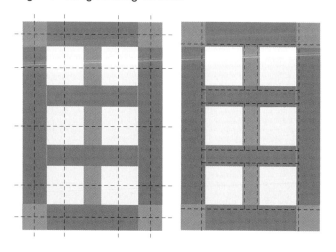

Making up the quilt

1 You will need to wash and iron your gingham fabric before cutting it to size to allow for shrinkage. Following the plan on the left, the centre section of the quilt is sewn together in horizontal strips before the outer border is added. With right sides together, and sewing on the wrong side, join the duck panel, piece B and the rabbit panel together, with a 1cm (⅜in) seam allowance. Repeat for the bear, piece B and the horse. Finally, join the the lamb, piece B and the zebra. Iron the strips on the wrong side, pressing the seams flat. Join the three strips together with piece A between each. Iron, pressing the seams flat. Sew piece D on to either side of the completed centre section. Iron, pressing the seams flat. Sew F on to either end of piece C, then sew the strip to the top of the centre panel. Repeat for the bottom. Iron, pressing the seams flat.

2 You now have three layers: the assembled top, with six cross stitched panels; the cotton batting; and the backing fabric D. Lay the backing fabric wrong side up on a big table or the floor and gently smooth out any wrinkles, and pick off any ends of cotton. Gently lay the batting over the top of the backing fabric and again pick off any cotton ends. Lay the assembled top right side up over the wadding. Smooth it gently and check that the edges of the backing, batting and top are all correctly matched.

3 Keeping the assembled quilt flat on the floor or table, pin through all three layers of fabric starting at the centre of the quilt, and then every 30cm (12in) or so across the surface. Thread your needle with a length of tacking cotton long enough to reach right across the quilt. Sew a series of grid lines across the quilt, and a row of stitches around the edge to hold the layers together (see diagram on the left).

This pretty nursery quilt is the perfect gift for a new born baby. When the baby becomes a toddler the quilt can be used to decorate the bedroom wall.

4 Thread your sewing needle with two strands of mauve stranded cotton (floss). Outline each of the cross stitched squares with a row of running stitches, 6mm (1/4in) outside the edge of the fabric. Stitch around each of the gingham panels in the same way (see below). Start and finish the stitching with a knot which should be pulled into the batting layer.

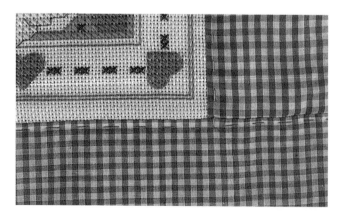

Running stitches have been used around the fabric pieces to hold the layers together.

5 Trim the wadding and the backing fabric level with the top of the quilt. Join the four lengths of fabric E together to make a continuous strip to bind the edge of the quilt. Fold the binding in half lengthways, right sides out and press. Working on the front of the quilt, and starting in the middle of one side, align the raw edges of the quilt and the binding and sew the layers together with a 2cm (3/4in) seam allowance. Sew as far as the first corner. Finish off the thread. Fold the binding over and continue around each side, stopping just short of where you started. Join the binding ends together, and then finish sewing the binding to the quilt.

6 Turn the binding over on to the reverse side of the quilt and sew it by hand along the edge with small, neat stitches. Remove the tacking stitches. Your quilt is now ready to use. Hand wash the quilt when it becomes dirty, and drip-dry outside in the breeze.

Bootees

The ready-made bootees used in this project have a front panel made from 14 count Aida fabric. The designs can also be stitched on to Aida, and then attached to a pair of bootees using Bondaweb

- *White bootees with a 14 count Aida panel*
- *DMC stranded cotton (floss) in the colours listed in the key*
- *Tapestry needle, No 24*

1 Carefully remove the ribbon from the bootees. Mark the centre front of each bootee with a tacking stitch. Work the design from the centre out following the chart and key on page 22. Use two strands of stranded cotton (floss) for the cross stitch and one strand for the backstitch.

2 Thread the ribbon back into each bootee and tie in a bow.

Sipper Cup

Depending on the size of the sipper cup you are using you may have to extend the design by repeating it again to completely cover the plastic canvas insert

- *sipper cup complete with cream 14 count plastic canvas insert 6.25cm (2½in diameter)*
- *DMC stranded cotton (floss) in the colours listed in the key*
- *Tapestry needle, No 24*

1 Slide the plastic canvas partly out of the cup and with a pencil mark the place where the canvas ends overlap. Extend the line from the top to the bottom edge of the canvas. Mark the centre point (top to bottom) on the line.

2 Start stitching at the point marked with a pencil line on the canvas, which is shown by an arrow on the chart on page 22 . Keep stitching until you get to the other end of the plastic canvas – you may have to extend the design by repeating part of it again. Use two strands of stranded cotton (floss) for the cross stitch, one strand for the backstitch on the teddy, chequered panel, ducks and ribbon and two on the remainder of the design. The french knots are made using one strand. When complete, slide the stitched canvas back into the cup, and snap on the lid.

Hooded Baby Towel

⊿ Ⴤ ⊥ ⬂ ⊙ ⬀ ⬂ ◆ ⊞ Ⅽ ⬆

A ready-made baby towel with an Aida panel can be used for this project, or you may prefer to make your own following the instructions given below

- White Aida fabric, 14 count 32.5x32.5cm (13x13in)
- White cotton towelling 76x76cm (30x30in)
- DMC stranded cotton (floss) in the colours listed in the key
- Tapestry needle, No 24
- White cotton bias binding 3.6m (4yds)
- White sewing thread

1 Fold the Aida fabric in half corner to corner to make a triangle. Cut the fabric on the fold to make two triangles.

2 Machine stitch bias binding along the bottom (longest side) of one Aida triangle. You will only need one Aida triangle for this project.

3 Pin the Aida triangle in one corner of the towelling square.

4 Fold the towelling in four, bringing the corners together. Use sharp scissors to carefully round off the points at the corners of the towelling. Cut through all the layers together, including the Aida, so that the corners are identical.

5 Pin, tack, then machine stitch bias binding around the four corners of the towelling. Take care that the Aida triangle in one corner of the towelling is in the correct position as you stitch.

Stitching the elephant design

1 Mark the centre of the Aida triangle with tacking stitches. Mount the fabric in an embroidery hoop, so that the tacking stitches are in the centre of the hoop.

2 Work the design from the centre out following the chart and key on page 23. Use two strands of stranded cotton (floss) for the cross stitch.

3 Backstitch the ribbon holding the hearts and the tuft of hair on the elephant's head using two strands of stranded cotton (floss), and the rest of the design using one strand.

4 Stitch the smaller heart motif in the bottom left and right corners of the Aida triangle.

5 Make french knots using one strand of white stranded cotton (floss) on each rain drop.

These stitched baby accessories are very practical as well as fun. The hooded baby towel, bootees and cup are sure to make bath and feeding time more enjoyable for both mum and baby.

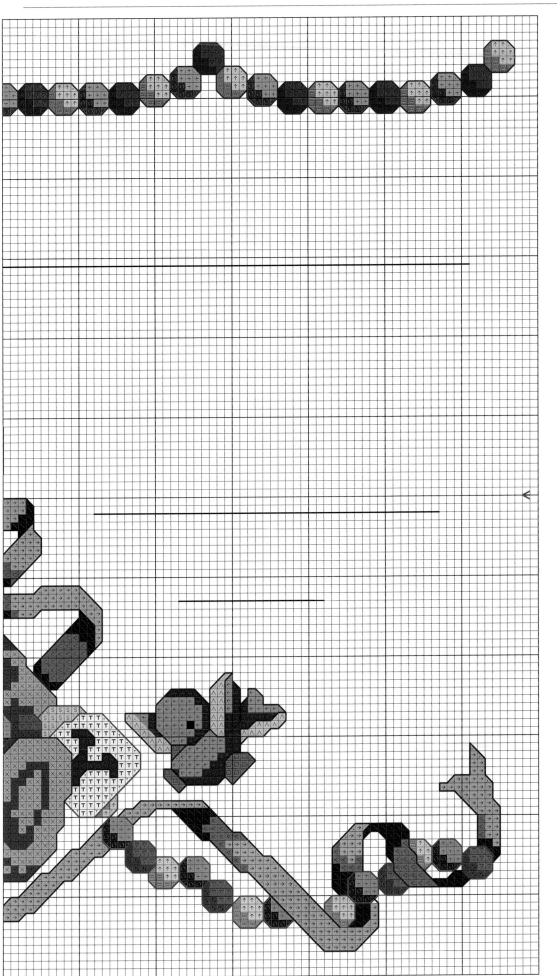

Toy Box Sampler

DMC stranded cotton (floss)

⊡	Blanc	Backstitch	
N	209	◪	209
Ⅱ	211	◪	310
■	310	◪	347
■	347	◪	350
◢	350	◪	351
▣	351	◪	434
←	352	◪	435
∧	353	◪	909
■	434	◪	3765
▤	435	French knots	
T	712	◉	Blanc
Y	726		
×	738		
S	739		
U	747		
▨	783		
■	909		
◀	912		
−	951		
→	954		
▤	956		
↑	957		
∩	3341		
I	3752		
◉	3765		
+	3766		

Horse

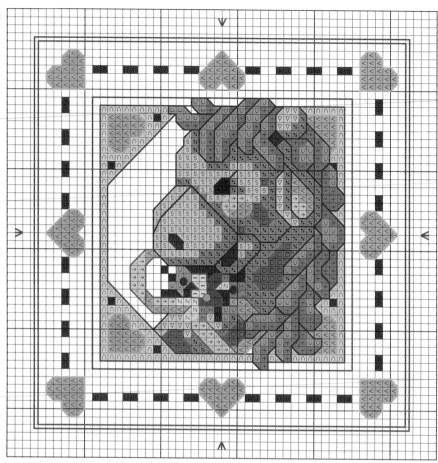

Bear

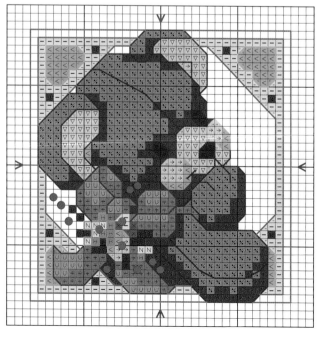

Duck

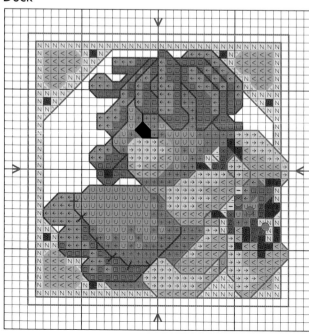

Rabbit

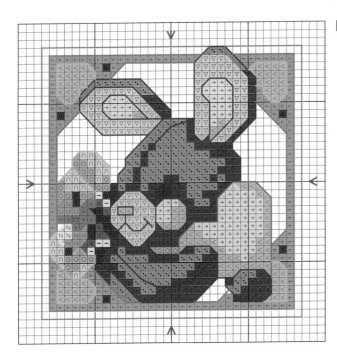

Baby Quilt

DMC stranded cotton (floss)

	Blanc	Backstitch	
⊡	208	⊘	208
H	209	⊘	209
N	211	⊘	310
■	310	⊘	351
⊡	351	⊘	435
∩	369	⊘	470
4	415	⊘	518
⊠	435	⊘	743
⊡	437	⊘	801
▦	470	⊘	899
✕	518	⊘	954
S	739	⊘	3731
+	743	⊘	3772
U	744	French knots	
–	747	◉	351
→	776	●	435
▦	801	◉	518
<	899	◉	743
▽	951	◉	744
○	954		
←	3341		

Zebra

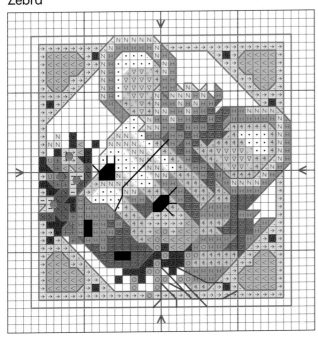

Lamb

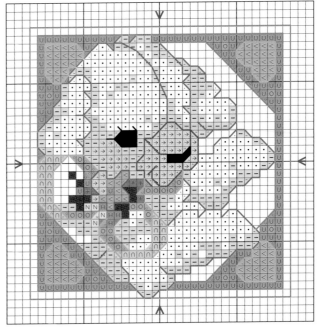

Sipper Cup

DMC stranded cotton (floss)		Backstitch		French knots	
H	209	◪	310	●	310
■	310	◪	351	●	3765
I	351	◪	553		
▨	553	◪	632		
+	726	◪	911		
=	776	◪	783		
∿	783	◪	954		
Z	894	◪	956		
■	911	◪	3765		
/	950				
C	954				
II	956				
↓	3064				
S	3341				
U	3765				
%	3766				

Bootees

DMC stranded cotton (floss)		Backstitch	
■	310	◪	310
←	321		
O	368	**French knots**	
+	726	◉	3341
H	956		
S	3341		
▲	3607		

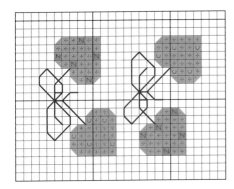

Hooded Baby Towel

DMC stranded cotton (floss)

·	Blanc	
+	224	
■	310	
∨	318	
◇	322	
⋋	415	
↗	552	
Ν	744	
⊿	826	
C	954	
F	3774	

Backstitch
⊿	414
⊿	552
⊿	826

French knots
○	Blanc

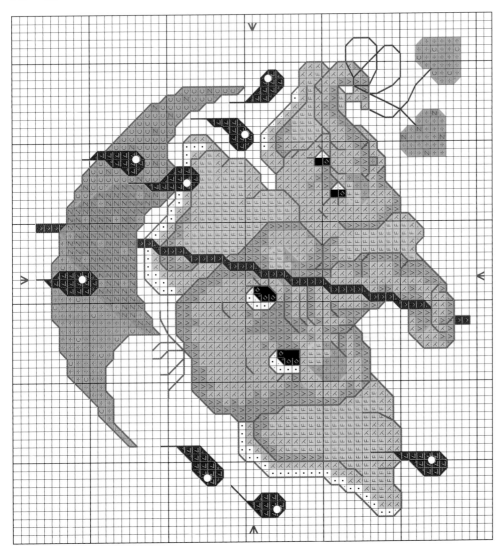

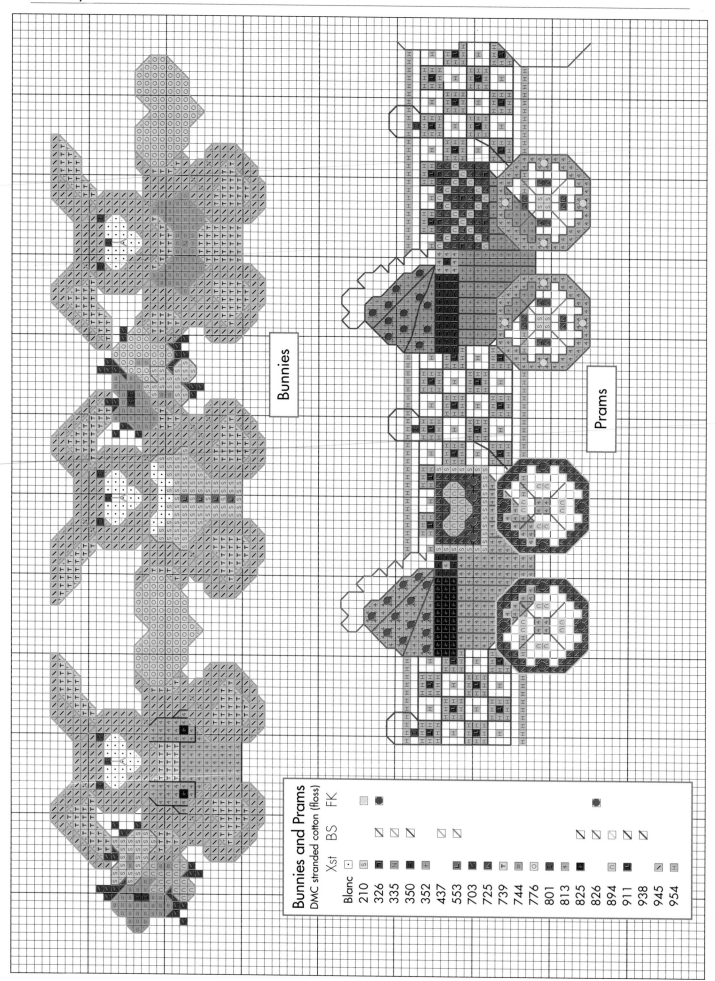

Bunnies

Prams

Bunnies and Prams
DMC stranded cotton (floss)

Xst BS FK

Blanc
210
326
335
350
352
437
553
703
725
739
744
776
801
813
825
826
894
911
938
945
954

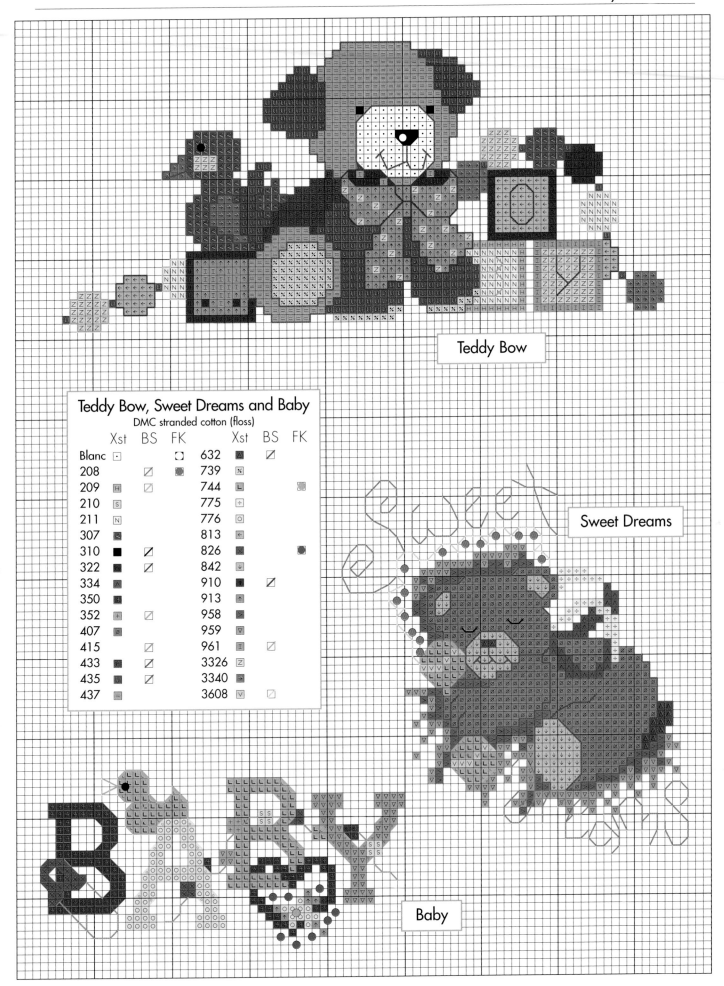

Teddy Bow

Teddy Bow, Sweet Dreams and Baby
DMC stranded cotton (floss)

	Xst	BS	FK		Xst	BS	FK
Blanc	·		◠	632	▲	◲	
208		◲	●	739	⊠		
209	H	◲		744	L		▦
210	S			775	+		
211	N			776	○		
307	◪			813	←		
310	■	◲		826	⊠		●
322	▦	◲		842	↓		
334	▲			910	▦	◲	
350	▦			913	↑		
352	+	◲		958	▶		
407	◙			959	▽		
415		◲		961	I	◲	
433	▦	◲		3326	Z		
435	U	◲		3340	◗		
437	▭			3608	∇	◲	

Sweet Dreams

Baby

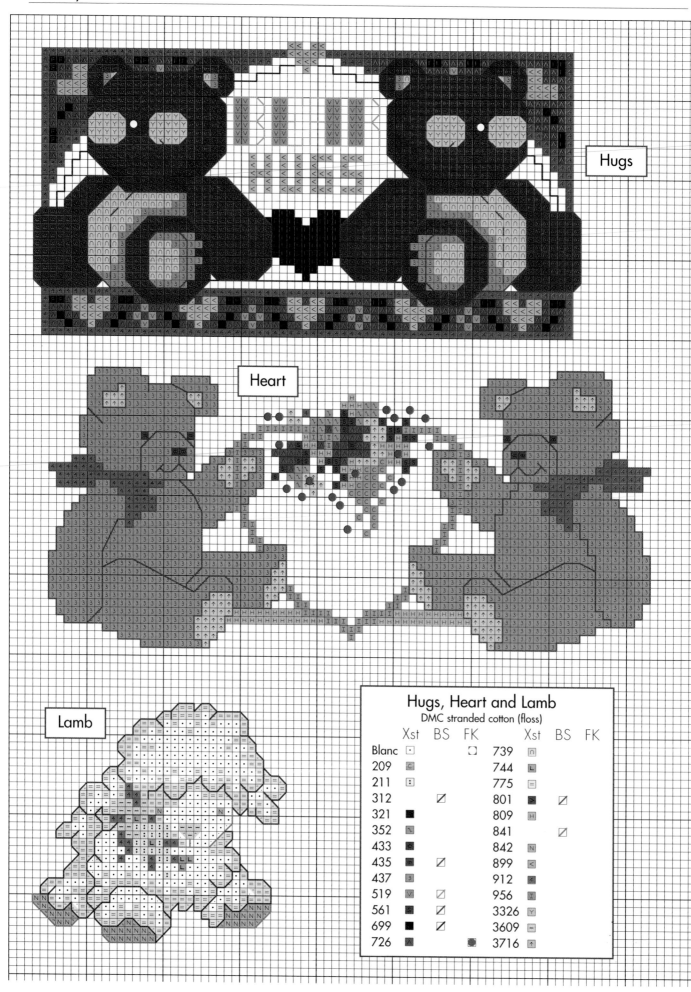

Hugs

Heart

Lamb

Hugs, Heart and Lamb
DMC stranded cotton (floss)

	Xst	BS	FK		Xst	BS	FK
Blanc	·		⌐	739	⌂		
209	C			744	L		
211	:			775	=		
312		⁄		801	■	⁄	
321	■			809	H		
352	↘			841		⁄	
433	▨			842	N		
435	▦	⁄		899	<		
437	3			912	▦		
519	V	⁄		956	I		
561	S	⁄		3326	Y		
699	■	⁄		3609	=		
726	▲		●	3716	↑		

Teddy Border

Teddy Checker

Teddy Posy

Teddies – Border, Checker and Posy
DMC stranded cotton (floss)

	Xst	BS	FK		Xst	BS	FK
310	■	◪		818	→		
322		◪		911		◪	
367	▨	◪	●	912	◪		
402	H			951	C		
436	▦			954	<		
553	▨			955	N	◪	
726	◪			956	⊠		
738	F			957	Σ		
739	▨			975		◪	
744	▤			3325	+		
783	▨	◪		3326	I		
800	4			3712	▨		◉
801	▨	◪		3766	▨		

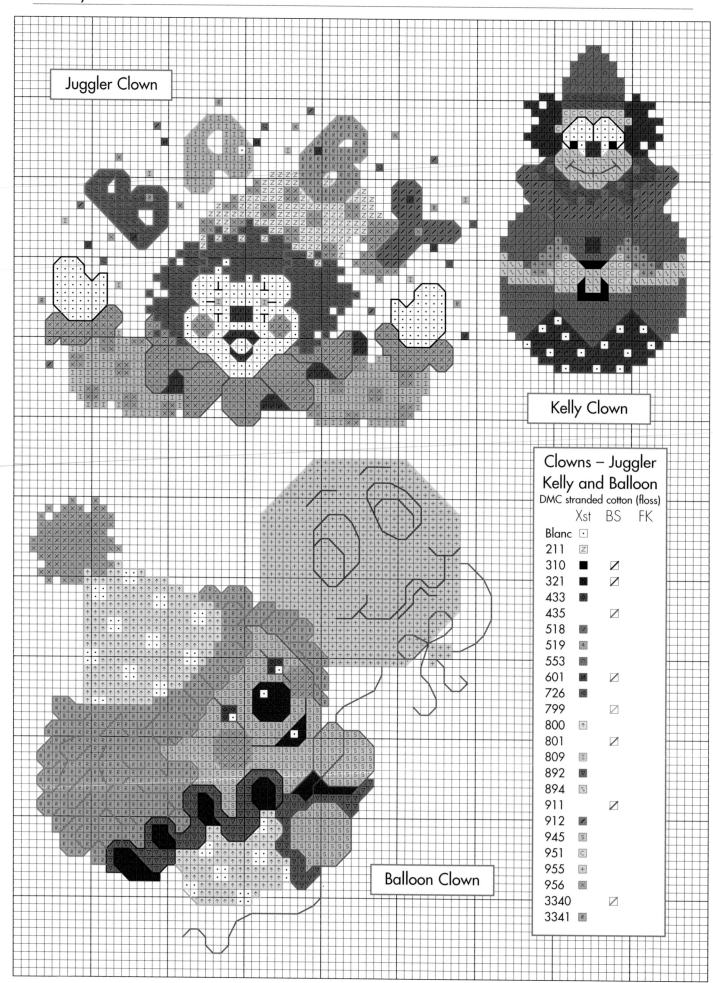

Juggler Clown

Kelly Clown

Balloon Clown

Clowns – Juggler
Kelly and Balloon
DMC stranded cotton (floss)

	Xst	BS	FK
Blanc	·		
211	Z		
310	■	╱	
321	▨	╱	
433	▩		
435		╱	
518	◪		
519	4		
553	n		
601	◪	╱	
726	◁		
799		╱	
800	↑		
801		╱	
809	I		
892	⊽		
894	◸		
911		╱	
912	◪		
945	S		
951	C		
955	+		
956	⊠		
3340		╱	
3341	℞		

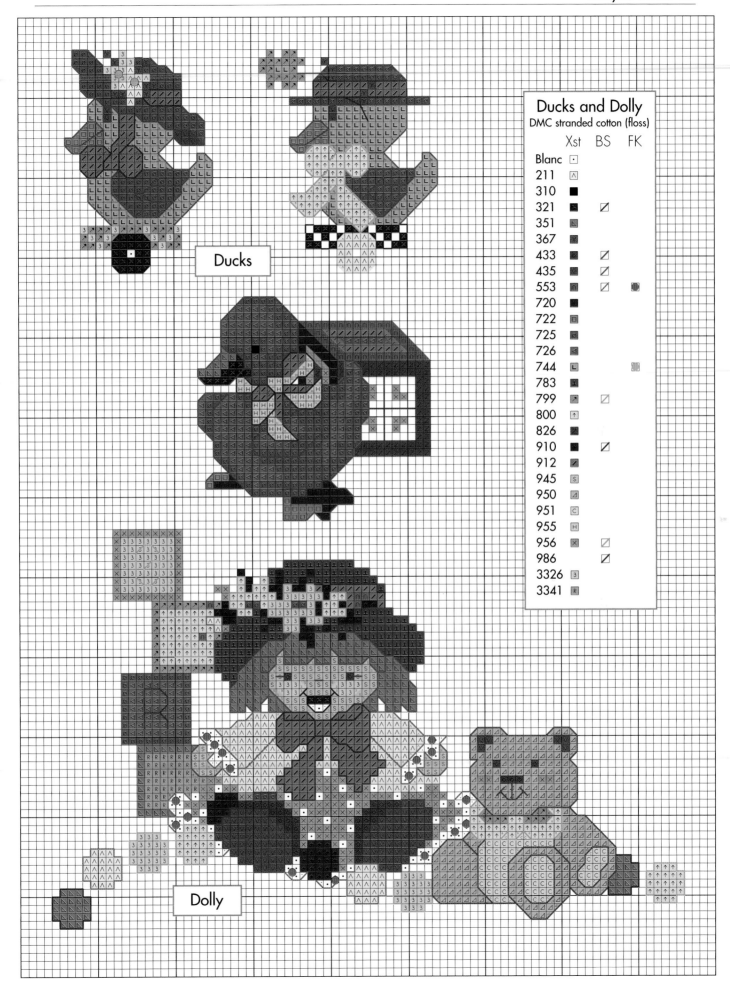

Ducks

Dolly

Ducks and Dolly
DMC stranded cotton (floss)

	Xst	BS	FK
Blanc	·		
211	⌃		
310	■		
321	▨	╱	
351	◩		
367	▦		
433	▩	╱	
435	▨	╱	
553	◨	╱	●
720	◪		
722	▢		
725	◉		
726	◁		
744	L		▨
783	⊥		
799	↗	╱	
800	↑		
826	▨		
910	■	╱	
912	◪		
945	S		
950	◢		
951	C		
955	H		
956	✕	╱	
986		╱	
3326	3		
3341	R		

Home Sweet Home

As we all know, there is no place quite like home. So what nicer way to show our love and respect for the place we live than to make a special sampler. The beautiful sampler in this chapter features white doves and the words "peace be unto this house", a sentiment that we all hope is present in our homes and those of the people we love. The tea cosy, pansy clock and heart key ring are perfect for giving to friends and family as house warming gifts. The home shelf makes a nice addition to any hallway; your keys can be attached to the heart shaped key ring which is then hung from the shelf. The house and pineapple designs have been stitched on linen, and then made into fragrant heart shaped sachets filled with potpourri. They can then be used to add fragrance to your linen drawer or wardrobe

Follow the instructions on the next page for working this beautiful sampler, which is stitched on ivory coloured Cashel linen over two threads of fabric.

Peace Sampler

To make the peace sampler into a picture, stitch the doves leaving off the trellis border edge and lettering

- *Ivory Zweigart Cashel linen, 28 count 38x30cm (15x12in)*
- *DMC stranded cotton (floss) in the colours listed in the key*
- *Tapestry needle, No 24*
- *Picture frame of your choice*

1 Mark the centre of your linen fabric with tacking stitches and oversew around the edges to prevent fraying. Mount the fabric in a frame or embroidery hoop. Work the peace sampler from the centre out following the chart and key on pages 40 and 41.

2 Use three strands of stranded cotton (floss) for the cross stitch, one strand for the green veins on the leaves, and two strands for the remainder of the backstitch and the french knots around the flowers. Each stitch on the chart should be worked over two threads of the fabric.

Framing the sampler

1 When the design is complete, wash and press it following the finishing instructions on page 124. Take your work to a professional picture framer for mounting and framing, or frame it yourself following the instructions on page 124.

Heart Key Ring

This heart design can also be used as a greetings card for Valentines day, or a gift tag to decorate a wedding gift

- *Ivory Zweigart Cashel linen, 28 count 8.75x6cm (3¹/₂x2¹/₄in)*
- *DMC stranded cotton (floss) in the colours listed in the key*
- *Plastic key ring with a design area of 7x4.5cm (2³/₄x1³/₄in)*
- *Tapestry needle, No 24*

1 Mark the centre of your fabric and oversew the edges to prevent them fraying. Work from the centre out, following the chart and key on page 45. Use three strands of stranded cotton (floss) for the cross stitch and two for the backstitch, working over two threads of fabric. Wash and press the design following the instructions on page 124. Cut the fabric to the same size as the paper template supplied with the key ring. Insert the design and snap the key ring

House Heart Sachet

To give your clothes a nice smell, add a few drops of your favourite essential oil to the wadding in the sachet, and then hang the sachet on a coat hanger in your wardrobe

- *White 25 count Zweigart Dublin linen 26x11cm (10½x4¼in)*
- *DMC stranded cotton (floss) as listed in the key*
- *Tapestry needle, No 24*
- *White sewing thread*
- *Toy stuffing*
- *Sewing thread and needle*
- *Small sachet of potpourri*
- *Length of piping cord, raffia*

1 Cut the linen rectangle in half so that you have two pieces 13x11cm (5¼x4¼in). Mark the centre on one piece of linen, then oversew the edges. Work the design from the centre out, following the chart and key on page 43. Use three strands of stranded cotton (floss) for the cross stitch, and two for the backstitch and french knots, working each stitch over two threads of the fabric. Wash and press the design following the instructions on page 124.

2 Using the house heart outline on page 123 as a guide, and with the design central, cut the shape from the stitched linen fabric. Cut the same heart shape from the other rectangle of linen.

3 Place the two heart shaped fabric pieces together, with the stitching facing inwards. To make the hanger, insert a folded length of piping cord between the two layers, so that the ends of the cord are level with the fabric edges. Sew around the edges of the heart shape with a 6mm (¼in) seam allowance. Leave a small gap on one side for turning.

4 Turn the heart through the gap to the right side. Stuff the shape with toy stuffing, inserting the potpourri sachet in the centre. Sew up the gap. Wrap raffia around the hanger, finishing with a bow at the top of the heart. Hold the bow in place with a few small stitches.

Home Panel

The cross stitched panel has been framed in the recess at the top of a ready-made display shelf. To do this, cut a piece of mounting board slightly larger than the recess, lace the stitching over the board, and then glue the panel in place

- *White Aida fabric, 14 count 10x16.5cm (4x6½in)*
- *DMC stranded cotton (floss) in the colours listed in the key*
- *Tapestry needle, No 24*
- *Display shelf and mounting board*

1 Mark the centre of the Aida fabric with tacking stitches, and oversew the edges. Work the design from the centre out, following the chart and key on page 42. Use three strands of stranded cotton (floss) for the cross stitch, one strand to outline the letters, and two strands for the ribbon and the saying.

2 Wash and press the stitching following the finishing instructions on page 124.

3 The home design can be used in a card, or mounted on to a rectangle of board and displayed in the recess of a wooden display shelf.

Small Heart Picture

Almost any part of a cross stitch design can be stitched and mounted in a small frame. Use the additional chart pages at the end of each chapter in this book for inspiration

- *White Aida fabric, 14 count 4x4cm (1½x1 ½in)*
- *DMC stranded cotton (floss) in the colours listed in the key*
- *Wooden frame with a design area of no more than 2x2cm (¾in x¾in)*

1 Stitch the small red heart following the chart and key on page 43. Use two strands of stranded cotton (floss) for the cross stitch.

2 Wash and press your design and then mount it in a small wooden frame.

This useful wooden shelf with its central cross stitch panel can be stitched using the chart and key on page 42. The heart sachets are filled with fragrant potpourri.

Is where you hang your heart

Heart Key Ring

This key ring design is quick-to-stitch, so it will also make a good subject for wedding favours, or even Christmas gift tags

- White Aida fabric, 14 count 6.25x6.25cm (2½x2½in)
- DMC stranded cotton (floss) in the colours listed in the key
- Plastic key ring with a design area of 4.5x4.5cm (1¾x1¾in)
- Tapestry needle, No 24

1 Mark the centre of your fabric and oversew the edges. Work from the centre out, following the chart and key on page 43. Use three strands of stranded cotton (floss) for the cross stitch, and two for the backstitch and french knots. Cut the fabric to the same size as the template supplied with the key ring. Insert the design, and snap the key ring shut.

Pineapple Heart Sachet

To make your linen drawer smell nice, fill the pineapple sachet with potpourri and place it in the drawer between the layers of clothing and sheets

- White Zweigart Dublin linen, 25 count 23x10cm (9x4in)
- DMC stranded cotton (floss) as listed in the key
- Tapestry needle, No 24
- White sewing thread and needle
- Toy stuffing
- Small sachet of potpourri
- White 1cm (³/8in) lace, 30cm (12in)

1 Cut the linen in half so that you have two pieces of fabric 11.5x10cm (4½x4in). Mark the centre of one piece of linen, and then oversew the edges. Work the design from the centre out, following the chart and key on page 42. Use three strands of stranded cotton (floss) for the cross stitch, and two for the backstitch and french knots, working each stitch on the chart over two threads of the fabric.

3 Cut out and then assemble the pineapple heart sachet in the same way as the house heart, using the template on page 123 as a guide. Leave a small gap at the top to add a hanger.

4 Make the hanger from a length of twisted fabric or upholstery cord. Fold it in half and push the ends in the gap left at the top of the heart. Sew up the gap. Sew white lace around the edge of the heart.

Roses Tea Cosy

Gold ribbon has been used on the tea cosy front to add extra interest. The ribbon is attached using small running stitches (see photograph below)

- *Ivory Zweigart Cashel linen, 28 count 24x30cm (9½x12in)*
- *Blue and cream striped chintz fabric 40x30cm (15¾x12in)*
- *Cream calico 24x96cm (9½x38in)*
- *2oz wadding 24x60cm (9½x24in)*
- *Cream ribbon 10cm (4in)*
- *DMC stranded cotton (floss) in the colours listed in the key*
- *Gold 3mm (⅛in) satin ribbon 56cm (22in)*
- *White sewing thread*
- *Tapestry needle, No 24*
- *Sewing needle, pins, large eyed bodkin*

1 Mark the centre of the linen, and oversew the edges in the same way as for the sampler. Mount the fabric in a frame or embroidery hoop. Work from the centre out following the chart and key on page 44. Use three strands of stranded cotton (floss) for the cross stitch, one strand for the backstitch and two strands for the lettering, working each stitch on the chart over two threads of fabric. Wash and press the stitched linen following the detailed instructions on page 124.

2 Thread a bodkin with yellow ribbon and tie a knot in the end. Working from the wrong side of the fabric, and following the chart on page 44 for position, push the needle up through a hole in the linen at the top of the pink heart located in the bottom left of your design. Push the needle down through a hole in the fabric on the edge of the bottom yellow rose. Continue in this way going up and down through the fabric, while following the chart on page 44 for position. Use pins to secure the ribbon as you work, finishing the ribbon on the wrong side of the fabric with a knot.

3 To anchor the ribbon to the linen, make a row of running stitches down the middle of the ribbon, using yellow stranded cotton (floss).

Making up the tea cosy

1 Enlarge the tea cosy templates on page 122 and 123 on a photocopier by 130%. Use the larger template to cut a tea cosy back from striped fabric, three inner pieces from calico, and two inner layers from wadding. Use the smaller template to cut the tea cosy front from the stitched linen.

2 Cut the remaining piece of striped fabric into two, lengthways. Join the pieces together to make one long strip, then fold in half lengthways. Gather up the fabric along the cut edge to make a frill. Stitch the frill on to the bottom of the tea cosy front, right sides together and with a 1cm (⅜in) seam allowance.

3 Lay one piece of the wadding flat on the table; on top of this lay the striped back, right side up; the tea cosy front with frill attached, facing down; one calico shape; and finally the other piece of wadding. Fold the cream ribbon in half and insert it between the striped fabric and the cosy front, so that the ribbon ends are level with the fabric edges. Sew the fabric sandwich together around the curve with a 1cm (⅜in) seam allowance, but leaving the bottom open.

4 Join the remaining two calico pieces together around the curved edge to make the inner lining, leaving the bottom open and a 12.5cm (5in) gap for turning.

5 Stitch the two sections together along the bottom edge. Turn the tea cosy right side out through the gap in the lining. Close the gap with a few small stitches. Push the lining up inside the tea cosy.

Pansy Clock

Pretty shades of mauve and pink have been used to stitch the pansies on this clock. If your clock is dark wood, you may want to lighten it with cream paint and then highlight the edges with aqua

- Ivory Zweigart Cashel linen, 28 count 16x12cm (6¼x4¾in)
- DMC stranded cotton (floss) in the colours listed in the key
- Tapestry needle, No 24
- Sudberry wooden carriage clock WS, design area 12.5x9cm (9x5in)
- Fray check, paint brush
- Cream and aqua acrylic paint

1 Mark the centre of the linen and oversew the edges of the fabric to prevent them fraying. Mount the fabric in a frame or embroidery hoop. Work the design from the centre out following the chart and key on page 45. Use three strands of stranded cotton (floss) for the cross stitch, two for the backstitch and the french knots, working each stitch on the chart over two threads of fabric. Wash and press your design following the finishing instructions on page 124.

2 Remove the movement and mounting board from the clock. Lay the stitching over the board, so that the centre point of the design is directly over the hole in the board. Wrap the excess fabric around the back of the board, and lace it in place (see page 124).

3 Cut a small hole in the fabric directly in line with the hole in the mounting board. Neaten the edges of the hole with fabric fray check.

Assembling the clock

1 To assemble the clock, place the mounted stitching on to the front of the clock. Push the movement through the hole in the centre, and attach the nut, washer and hands.

If your clock is dark wood, paint it with two coats of cream coloured acrylic paint to make it a lighter colour. When dry, use aqua paint to highlight the edges.

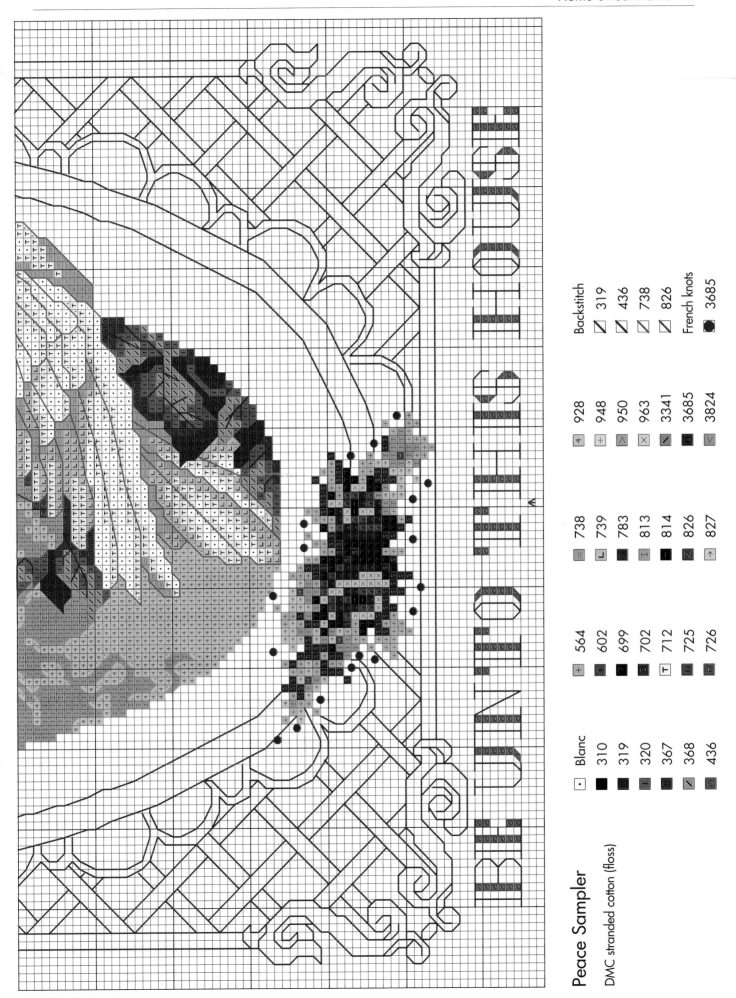

Peace Sampler

DMC stranded cotton (floss)

·	Blanc	
■	310	
▨	319	
⊤	320	
▨	367	
◣	368	
◉	436	

+	564	
◄	602	
⊿	699	
⊑	702	
⊤	712	
▨	725	
⊞	726	

▥	738	
⌐	739	
▦	783	
⊢	813	
▮	814	
▨	826	
↑	827	

◢	928	
⊹	948	
∧	950	
✕	963	
◪	3341	
◼	3685	
∨	3824	

Backstitch
⧄	319
⧄	436
⧄	738
⧄	826

French knots
●	3685

Home Panel

DMC stranded cotton (floss)

⊠	326		Backstitch
■	517	╱	326
▽	518	╱	435
⊠	519	╱	517
■	699	╱	699
N	701	╱	783
↑	744		French knots
−	745	◼	435
≡	783		
O	954		
U	961		
Z	3326		

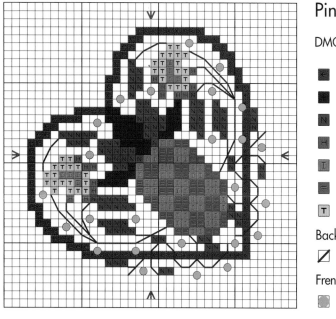

Pineapple Heart Sachet

DMC stranded cotton (floss)

◧	434
■	699
N	701
H	718
I	726
≡	783
T	3608

Backstitch

╱ 699

French knots

◼ 209

House Heart Sachet

DMC stranded cotton (floss)

■	326	Backstitch	
■	434	☑	701
■	517	☑	801
▽	518	French knots	
△	553	●	326
■	701	●	783
▬	783		
■	801		
○	954		
4	957		
∧	3779		

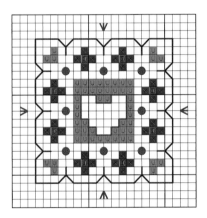

Heart Key Ring
and Small Heart Picture

DMC stranded cotton (floss)

■	326
■	726
⊍	961

Backstitch

☑ 326

☑ 701

French knots

● 518

Roses Tea Cosy

DMC stranded cotton (floss)

		Backstitch	
⊡	320	◻	367
▨	367	◻	801
+	368	◻	806
✕	597	◻	899
Y	598		Ribbon
◄	725	◻	Gold
▷	727		
S	783		
N	806		
▫	818		
O	899		

Heart Key Ring

DMC stranded cotton (floss)

U	210
S	368
H	597
◄	725
N	806
Z	818
✕	899
	Backstitch
◻	913

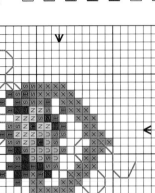

Pansy Clock

DMC stranded cotton (floss)

I	210
+	368
◄	725
▪	792
O	899
	Backstitch
◻	367
	French knots
▨	598

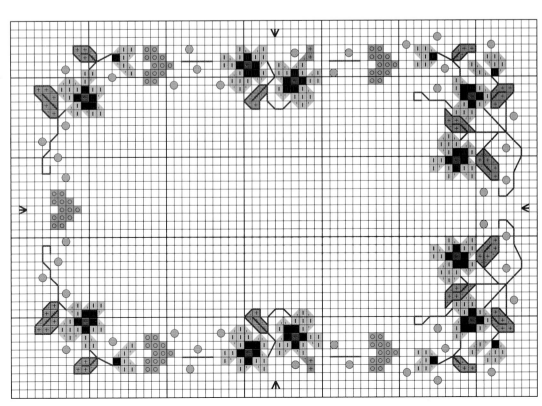

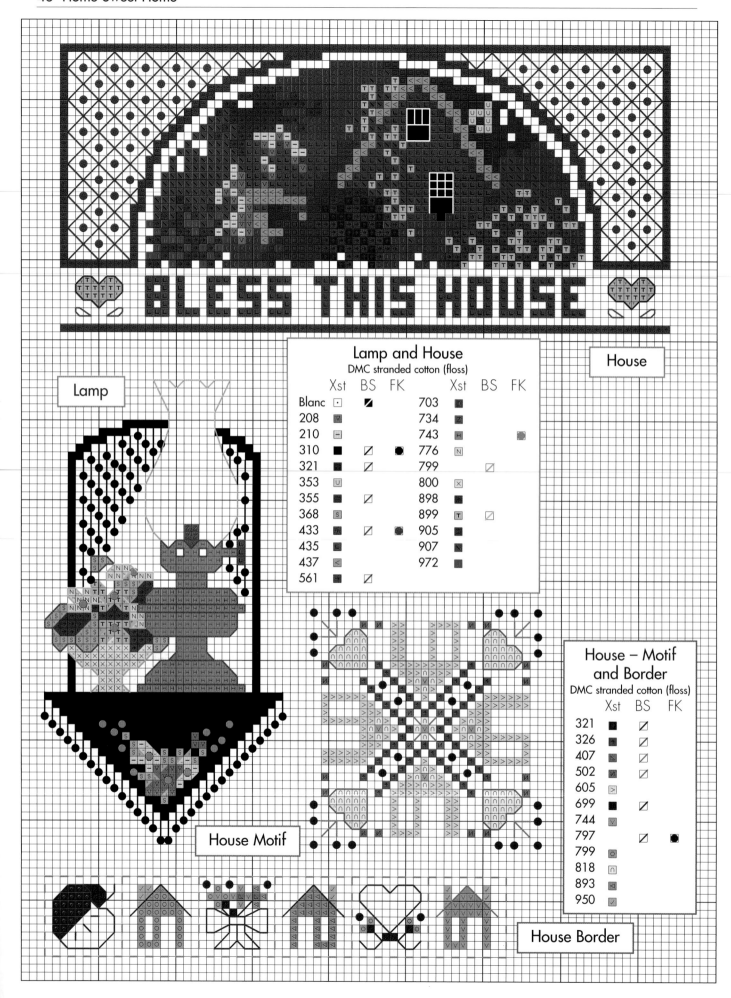

Lamp and House
DMC stranded cotton (floss)

	Xst	BS	FK		Xst	BS	FK
Blanc	·	◪		703	▦		
208	▨			734	▦		
210	−			743	H		▣
310	■	◪	●	776	N		
321	▨	◪		799		◪	
353	U			800	×		
355	▨	◪		898	▨		
368	S			899	T	◪	
433	▨	◪	●	905	▨		
435	L			907	▨		
437	<			972	▥		
561	▨	◪					

Lamp

House

House Motif

House – Motif and Border
DMC stranded cotton (floss)

	Xst	BS	FK
321	■	◪	
326	▨	◪	
407	▨	◪	
502	▨	◪	
605	▷		
699	■	◪	
744	▨		
797		◪	●
799	○		
818	∩		
893	◁		
950	▨		

House Border

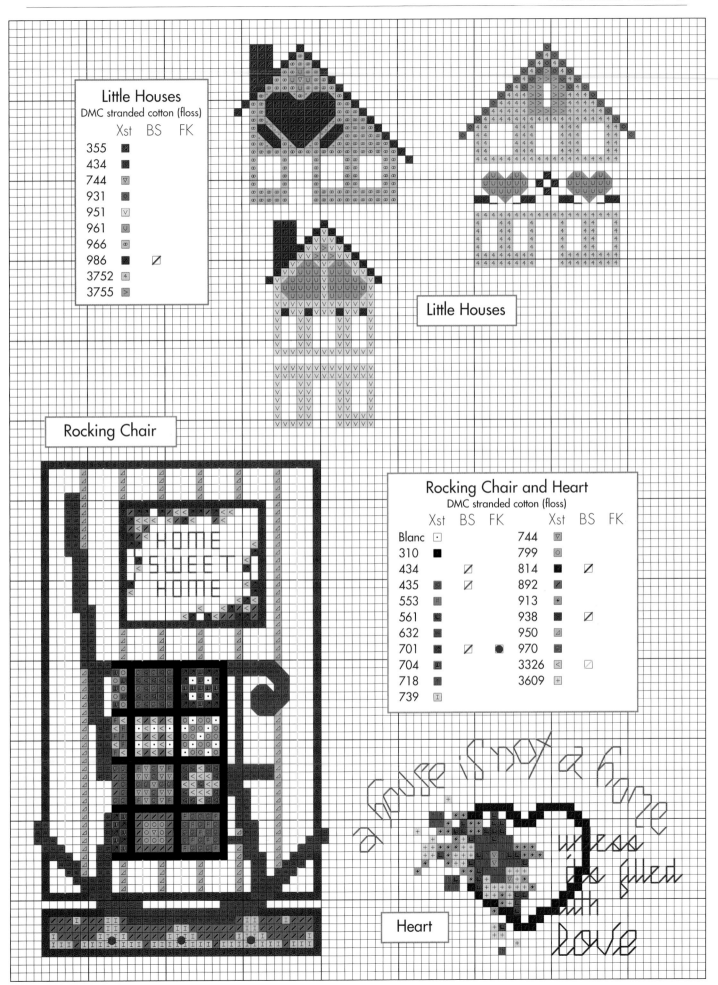

Little Houses
DMC stranded cotton (floss)

	Xst	BS	FK
355			
434			
744			
931			
951			
961			
966			
986			
3752			
3755			

Little Houses

Rocking Chair

Rocking Chair and Heart
DMC stranded cotton (floss)

	Xst	BS	FK		Xst	BS	FK
Blanc				744			
310				799			
434				814			
435				892			
553				913			
561				938			
632				950			
701				970			
704				3326			
718				3609			
739							

Heart

Love and Welcome
DMC stranded cotton (floss)

	Xst	BS	FK
208			
309			
310			
320			
414			
518			
519			
562			
632			
699			
726			
899			
912			
945			
954			
966			
3340			
3608			

Love

Welcome

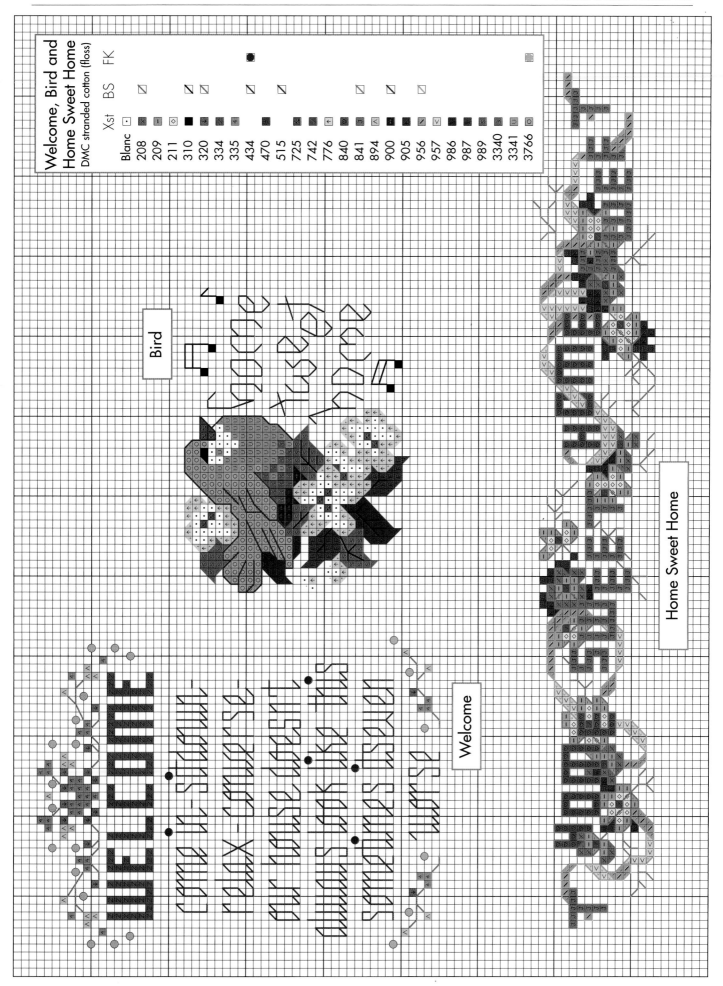

Welcome, Bird and Home Sweet Home
DMC stranded cotton (floss)

	Xst	BS	FK
Blanc	·		
208			
209			
211			
310			
320			
334			
335			
434			●
470			
515			
725			
742			
776			
840			
841			
894			
900			
905			
956			
957			
986			
987			
989			
3340			
3341			
3766			

Bird

Welcome

Home Sweet Home

Welcome

Welcome and Bless
DMC stranded cotton (floss)

	Xst	BS	FK		Xst	BS	FK
Blanc	·		◌	839	▦	⁄	
326	▨	⁄		898	▦	⁄	
754	⋀			909	▦	⁄	
783	◌	⁄		954	→		
813	и			3341	⊠	⁄	
825	▪	⁄		3708	↑		
826	S			3772		⁄	

Bless

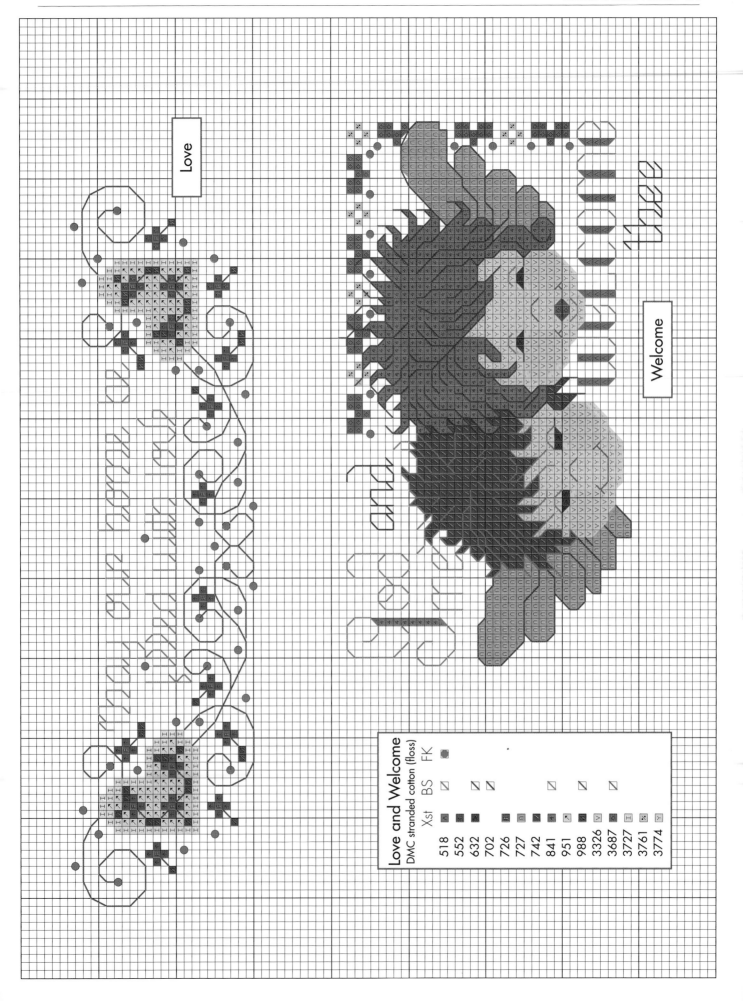

Love

Welcome

Love and Welcome
DMC stranded cotton (floss)

	Xst	BS	FK
518			
552			
632			
702			
726			
727			
742			
841			
951			
988			
3326			
3687			
3727			
3761			
3774			

Childhood Days

∧ Y ⊥ ↘ ● ↖ ◆ + C ↑

Castles in the sky, fairy dust, pixies, elves and goblins are all from the stories we love to hear when we are young. So why not capture the magic of childhood with this fairy-tale sampler, stitched in one shade of blue stranded cotton (floss), with beads and blending filament added to make it sparkle.

As well as fairy stories, children always enjoy the colour and razamataz of the circus, so the notice board with the clown panel, and colourful pin tops is just the thing to brighten a bedroom wall.

The circus is also the inspiration for the designs used on the scarf, gloves, greetings card, bag and key ring.

The teddy, fairy, dog and balloon birthday cards are quick and easy to stitch on ivory Aida, and on two of the cards there is space to add the child's age in cross stitch

This fairy-tale sampler is stitched in blue with blending filament and beads used to add sparkle. The chart can be found on pages 62 and 63.

Fairy-tale Sampler

Beads and blending filament are mixed with the stranded cotton to give this fairy-tale sampler lots of sparkle. Use the alphabet on page 121 to stitch your child's name

- *Cream Aida fabric, 14 count 42.5x35cm (17x14in)*
- *DMC stranded cotton (floss) – 3 skeins 809, 1 skein 792*
- *Kreinek Metallics blending filament colour 095 – 3 spools*
- *Mill Hill seed beads, blue 02026*
- *Tapestry needle, No 24*
- *Picture frame and mount of your choice*

1 Mark the centre of your Aida fabric and oversew around the edges to prevent fraying. Work the design from the centre out following the chart and key on pages 62 and 63. Use two strands of stranded cotton and one strand of blending filament for the cross stitch, and one strand of stranded cotton and two strands of blending filament for the backstitch and the french knots. Use the alphabet on page 121 to add the child's name. After the stitching is complete the beads are attached using two strands of 809 blue stranded cotton. Attach the bead with the first leg of the cross stitch, then anchor it in place with the second leg, allowing one strand to go either side of the bead. Follow the instructions on page 125 for finishing and framing your sampler.

Blending filament has been used with the stranded cotton (floss) to make the stitches shine.

Circus Fun Gift Card & Pin Tops

This jolly clown with his bright waistcoat and spotted tie has been made into a birthday card.
A fun pin top can be used to display the card on the child's notice board

- *Cream Aida fabric, 14 count 15x20.5cm (6x8in)*
- *Perforated paper, 14 count cream 10x10cm (4x4in)*
- *DMC stranded cotton (floss) in the colours listed in the key*
- *Tapestry needle, No 24*
- *Card with a 10x14.5cm (4x5¾in) oval aperture*
- *Large headed notice board pins*
- *Double-sided tape*

Stitching the clown card

1 Mark the centre of your Aida fabric with tacking stitches and mount the fabric in an embroidery hoop.

2 Work the design from the centre out following the chart and key on page 65. Use three strands of stranded cotton (floss) for the cross stitch, and one strand for the backstitch and the french knots.

3 Wash, then press your design following the instructions on page 125.

4 To mount the cross stitch in a card, first check that the stitching fits the window opening. Trim the fabric to fit the card.

5 Put small lengths of double-sided tape around the window opening on the inside of the card. Remove the backing paper from the tape. Lay the card on the design so that it is lined up in the window open-

The clown card has been stitched on to 14 count Aida fabric, and the pin top on perforated paper. Both are stitched using three strands of stranded cotton (floss).

ing of the card. Press the fabric in place. Fold one of the flaps in to cover the back of the card. Check that the card opens correctly before securing the flap with double-sided tape.

Stitching the pin tops

1 Hand hold the perforated paper while you stitch the four motifs following the chart and key on page 65. Use four strands of stranded cotton (floss) for the cross stitch and two for the backstitch. Where there is a half stitch, make a hole in the paper using a sharp needle before making the stitch.

2 Using small scissors cut around each motif, leaving one square of paper around the design.

3 Use a small piece of double-sided tape to attach each motif to the top of a pin.

Clown Notice Board

Any cork notice board can be used to display the clown design as long as it has a panel large enough at the top for holding the stitching

- Cream Aida fabric, 14 count 12.5x30cm (5x12in)
- DMC stranded cotton (floss) in the colours listed in the key
- Tapestry needle, No 24
- Cork notice board with a top picture panel
- Mount board, glue or double-sided tape

1 Mark the centre of your Aida fabric with tacking stitches and oversew around the fabric edges to prevent fraying. Mount the fabric in a frame or embroidery hoop.

2 Work the design from the centre out following the chart and key on pages 64 and 65. Use three strands of stranded cotton (floss) for the cross stitch, and one strand for the backstitch and the french knots.

Displaying your stitching

1 Wash and press the stitching following the instructions on page 125. Ask your picture framer to cut two pieces of mount board: one slightly smaller than the panel at the top of the cork board, and the other to fit snugly into the panel, with a 7.5x20.5cm (3x8in) hole cut in the centre to display the stitching.

2 Following the instructions on page 125, lace your design around the smaller piece of board.

3 Use glue or double-sided tape to attach the mount board with the cut-out to the front of the stitched, mounted panel. Secure the panel in to the space at the top of the notice board with tape or glue.

Bright cheerful wrapping paper has been glued to the mount board around the stitched panel.

Circus Animal Scarf and Tiger Gloves

Circus animals have been used to decorate a plain cream scarf and woollen gloves. The stitching is done on Aida fabric, and then attached to the gloves using Bondaweb

❧ *Cream Aida fabric, 14 count 7.5x7.5cm (3x3in) – for each design*
❧ *DMC stranded cotton (floss) in the colours listed in the key*
❧ *Wool scarf or length of woollen material*
❧ *Woollen gloves*
❧ *Cotton perle number 5, colour 321 red*
❧ *Vilene Bondaweb*
❧ *Tapestry needle, No 24*
❧ *Large eyed needle*
❧ *Fine sewing needle and cream thread*

1 Oversew the Aida edges to prevent fraying. Mount the fabric in an embroidery hoop.

2 Work each design on to the fabric following the chart and key on page 65. Use two strands of stranded cotton (floss) for the cross stitch, and one strand for the backstitch.

3 Wash and press your stitching following the instructions on page 125.

Making the scarf

1 Using a large eyed needle and red perle cotton to make a row of blanket stitches, approximately 6mm (1/4in) apart, around the edge of a scarf or length of woollen fabric (see page 124).

2 Lay your design face down on to your ironing board. On top of this place a piece of Bondaweb, adhesive side down. Fuse the Aida and Bondaweb together using a dry iron. Use small scissors to cut around the design, leaving one square of Aida around the edge of the stitching.

3 Remove the paper from the back of the Bondaweb, and position a motif on to one end of the scarf. Repeat on the other end of the scarf.

4 Cover the motifs with a damp cloth and press with a hot, dry iron to fuse them to the scarf.

5 To make the design even more secure, make a row of small buttonhole stitches around the edge of the fabric using a fine needle and cream thread.

Making the gloves

1 Use Bondaweb and buttonhole stitches to attach a tiger's head to the back of each glove in the same way as for the scarf.

Monkey Key Ring

To make sure your child doesn't lose his door key, attach it to this fun monkey key ring stitched in bright red, mauve and green

- ❧ Cream Aida fabric, 18 count 7.5x5cm (3x2in)
- ❧ DMC stranded cotton (floss)
- ❧ Plastic key ring with a design area of 7x4.5cm (2³/4x1³/4in)
- ❧ Tapestry needle, No 24

1 Use two strands of stranded cotton (floss) to stitch the cross stitch, and one strand for the backstitch and french knots using the chart and key on page 65. Cut the fabric to size, insert it in the key ring, and snap the back shut.

Elephant Bag

This pretty gingham bag can be used as a shoe bag, or by adding a waterproof lining it will make a very useful sponge bag.

- ❧ Cream Aida fabric, 14 count 12.5x30cm (5x12in)
- ❧ DMC stranded cotton (floss) in the colours listed in the key
- ❧ Cotton gingham fabric – one piece 15x24cm (6x9¹/2in), and one 42x24cm (16¹/2x 9¹/2in)
- ❧ Waterproof lining fabric 54x24cm (21¹/2x9¹/2in)
- ❧ Garden string or cord
- ❧ Tapestry needle, No 24
- ❧ White sewing thread and needle

1 To make sure the child's name will fit on to the Aida panel, the letters should be planned on graph paper before you cut the fabric. The Aida and the bag may have to be made wider if the child's name is very long. Cut out the Aida fabric and mark the centre with tacking stitches. Oversew around the edges then mount the fabric in a frame or embroidery hoop.

2 Work the design from the centre out following the chart and key on pages 64 and 65. Use three

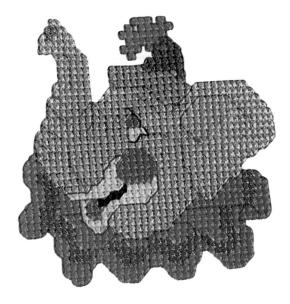

strands of stranded cotton (floss) for the cross stitch, and one strand for the backstitch.

Making the gingham bag

1 Wash and press the stitching following the instructions on page 125. To make the front and back of the bag, attach the smaller piece of gingham to the top edge of the stitched design with a 1cm (³⁄₈in) seam allowance. Attach the larger piece to the bottom edge in the same way. Neaten the seams by oversewing the edges. The bag front and back are now one complete length of fabric; when the bag is assembled the stitched panel will be roughly in the centre front of the bag.

2 On one short edge of the gingham fabric, turn over the top 1cm (³⁄₈in) to the wrong side of the fabric, and then turn over another 2.5cm (1in). Sew across the fabric to hold the double turning in place. Make another row of stitches 1cm (³⁄₈in) above the first to make a channel for holding the drawstring. Repeat at the other end of the fabric.

3 Fold the fabric in half so that the cross stitch is facing inwards. Stitch down both sides of the bag with a 1cm (³⁄₈in) seam allowance, leaving gaps on either side of the bag for the channels.

4 Thread a length of string or cord through the channel at the top of the bag, then tie the ends together in a knot. To make the drawstring stronger, thread a second length of string or cord through the same channel, taking it out on the opposite side of the bag. Pull up both lengths at the same time.

Happy Birthday Cards

These cute birthday cards stitched on to ivory coloured Aida, are suitable for boys and girls. On two of the cards the age of the child can be added using the chart on page 119

- Ivory Aida fabric, 14 count 15x10cm (6x4in)
- DMC stranded cotton (floss) in the colours listed in the key
- Tapestry needle, No 24
- Card with a 10x7cm (4x2³⁄₄) rectangular aperture for each card

1 Mark the centre of your Aida fabric with tacking stitches and oversew around the fabric edges to prevent fraying. Mount the fabric in an embroidery hoop.

2 Work the design from the centre out following the chart and key on pages 66 and 67.

3 Use two strands of stranded cotton (floss) for the cross stitch, and one strand for the backstitch and the french knots.

4 Wash and press your stitching following the instructions on page 125.

5 Mount each design in a card, following the instructions on page 82.

Ivory coloured Aida has been used for these birthday cards. One card has been designed for a girl, one for a boy and the other two say 'happy birthday'.

Fairy Tale Sampler

DMC stranded cotton (floss)

809 (2 strands)
095* (1 strand)

Backstitch
792 (1 strand)
095* (2 strands)

French knots
792 (1 strand)
095* (2 strands)

Beads
02026**

*Kreinik Metallics Blending Filament **Mill Hill seed beads

Circus Fun

DMC stranded cotton (floss)

·	Blanc	V	552	H	726		907
↑	209	+	553	∨	776		912
H	211	I	666	◄	782	▷	952
■	310	∪	676	⌐	783	+	954
□	335	+	680	L	798		
◣	351	I	702	◇	813		
▨	353	S	722	↓	891		
∩							

Backstitch

◢	310		702
◺	335		722
	351		783
	414		798
	434		891
	435		912
	444		
	552		
	666		

French knots

○	Blanc	●	666
●	310		726
	353		

◉	400	
↓	414	
←	415	
✕	434	
✕	435	
◹	437	
∪	444	

Special Boy Card

DMC stranded cotton (floss)

·	Blanc		Backstitch
■	310	⁄	310
U	407	⁄	601
◤	601	⁄	632
▤	632		French knots
✕	798	◯	Blanc
S	956	●	310
→	950	⬤	407
↑	957		
−	963		

Balloon Card

DMC stranded cotton (floss)

↑	743
−	813
✕	824
U	894
S	913

Backstitch

⁄	310
⁄	434
⁄	600
⁄	699
⁄	824

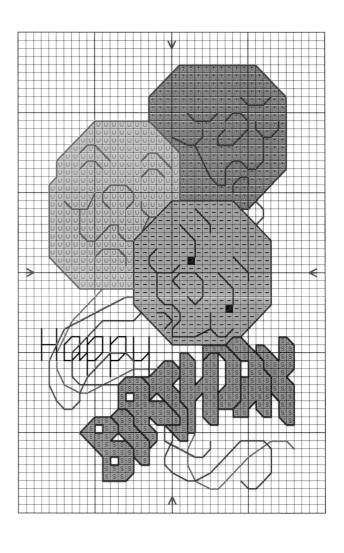

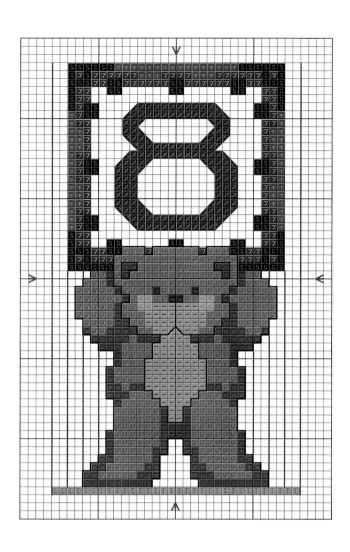

Bear Card

DMC stranded cotton (floss)

S	321	Backstitch	
7	444	⟋	519
I	519	⟋	632
	632		
4	912		
–	950		
X	995		
U	3064		
<	3354		
	3772		

Angel Card

DMC stranded cotton (floss)

–	434	Backstitch	
+	504	⟋	321
<	743	⟋	434
S	754	⟋	988
I	783	⟋	3687
–	988	French knots	
X	995	●	3687
↑	3688		
Z	3716		

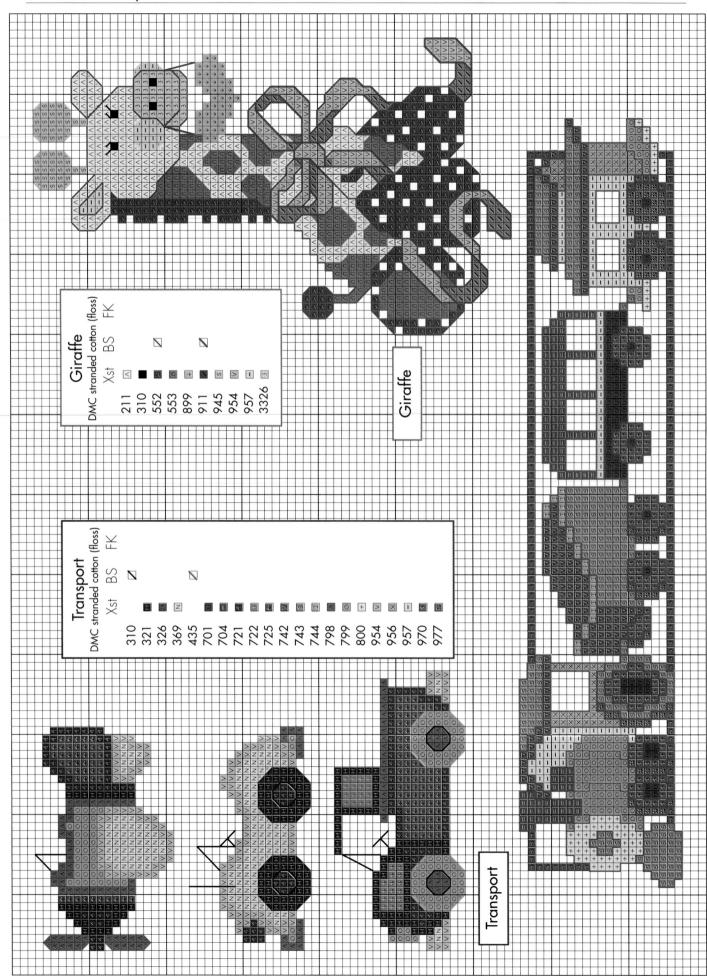

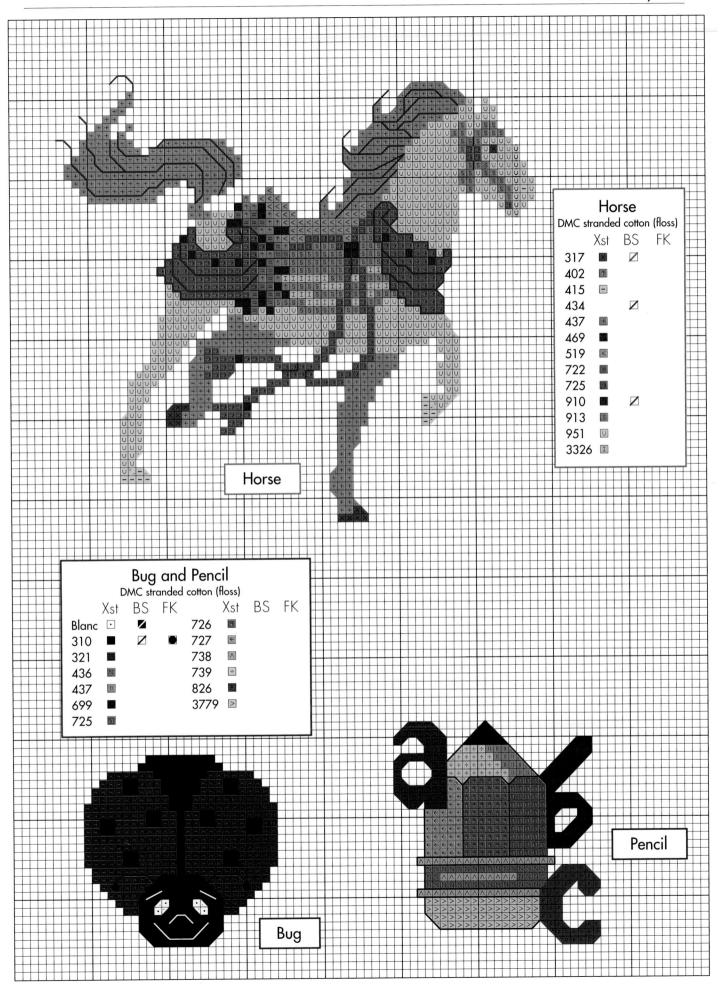

Horse

Horse
DMC stranded cotton (floss)

	Xst	BS	FK
317			
402			
415			
434			
437			
469			
519			
722			
725			
910			
913			
951			
3326			

Bug and Pencil
DMC stranded cotton (floss)

	Xst	BS	FK		Xst	BS	FK
Blanc				726			
310				727			
321				738			
436				739			
437				826			
699				3779			
725							

Pencil

Bug

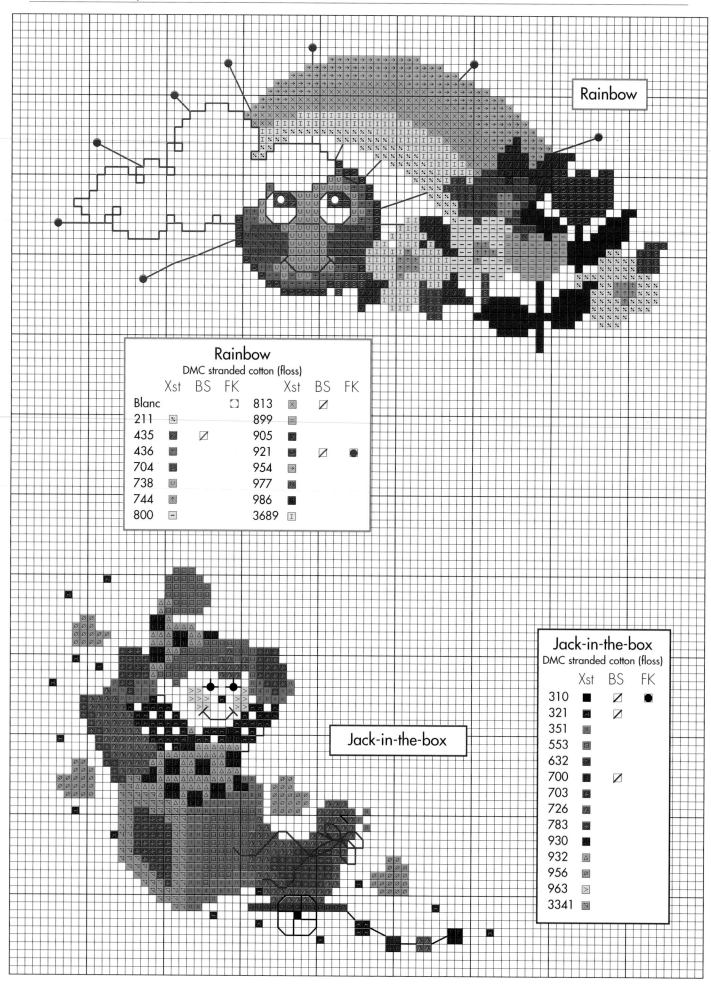

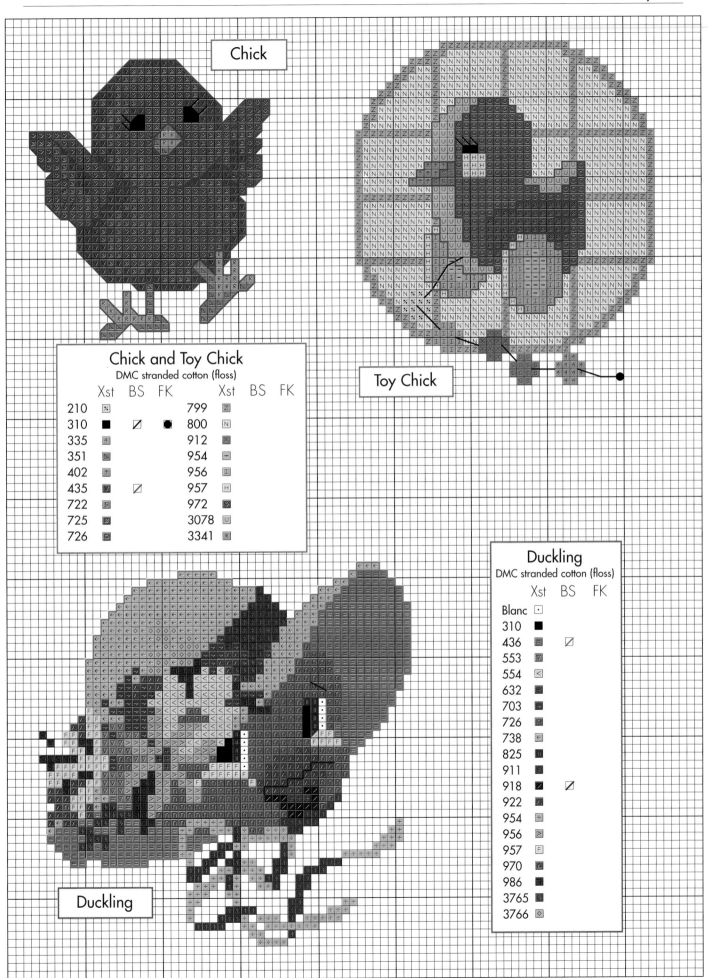

Chick

Toy Chick

Chick and Toy Chick
DMC stranded cotton (floss)

	Xst	BS	FK		Xst	BS	FK
210				799			
310				800			
335				912			
351				954			
402				956			
435				957			
722				972			
725				3078			
726				3341			

Duckling
DMC stranded cotton (floss)

	Xst	BS	FK
Blanc			
310			
436			
553			
554			
632			
703			
726			
738			
825			
911			
918			
922			
954			
956			
957			
970			
986			
3765			
3766			

Duckling

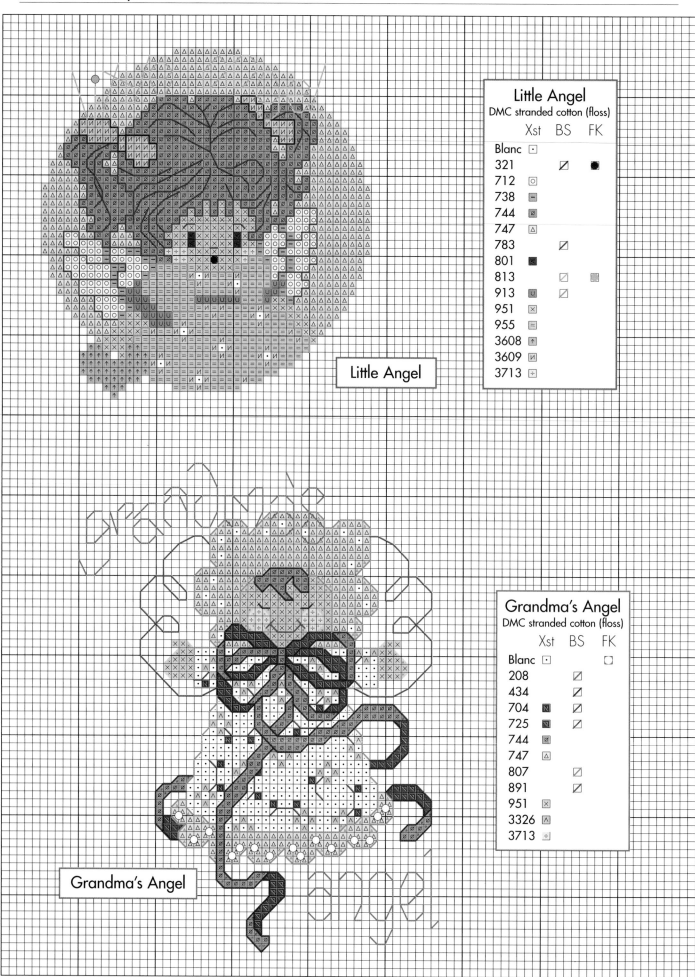

Little Angel

Little Angel
DMC stranded cotton (floss)

	Xst	BS	FK
Blanc	⊡		
321		◪	●
712	⊙		
738	⊟		
744	⊘		
747	△		
783		◪	
801	◼		
813		◪	◪
913	U	◪	
951	⊠		
955	⊟		
3608	↑		
3609	И		
3713	⊞		

Grandma's Angel

Grandma's Angel
DMC stranded cotton (floss)

	Xst	BS	FK
Blanc	⊡		◻
208		◪	
434		◪	
704	N	◪	
725	◩	◪	
744	⊘		
747	△		
807		◪	
891		◪	
951	⊠		
3326	Λ		
3713	⊞		

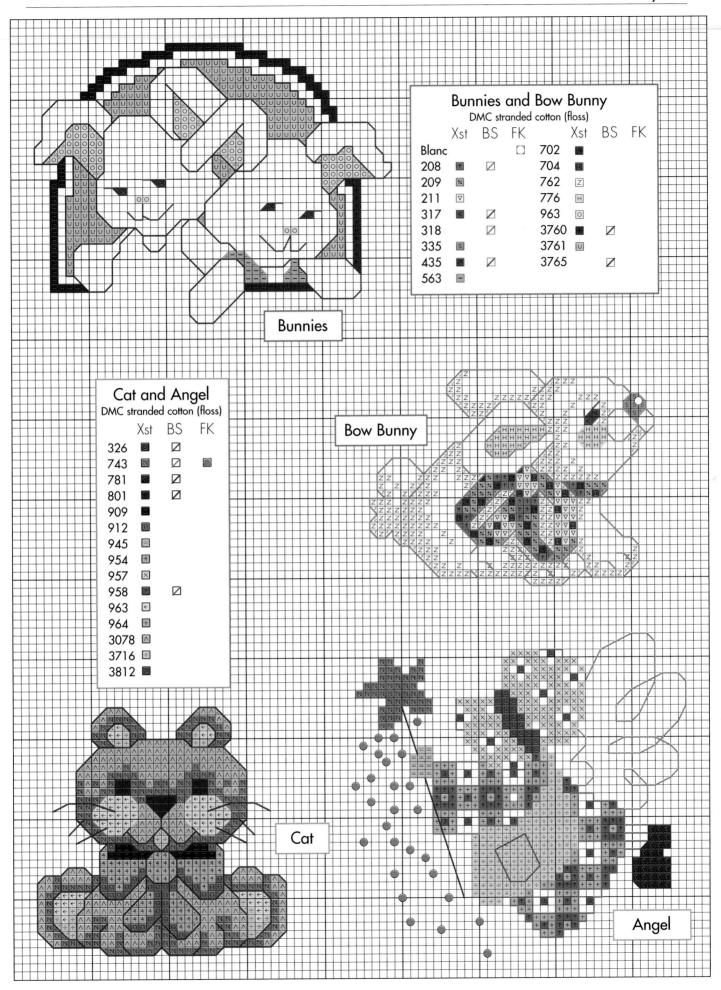

Bunnies and Bow Bunny
DMC stranded cotton (floss)

	Xst	BS	FK		Xst	BS	FK
Blanc			□	702	▓		
208	↑	∕		704	▣		
209	▨			762	▨		
211	▽			776	H		
317	▓	∕		963	○		
318	▨	∕		3760	▓	∕	
335	S			3761	U		
435	▓	∕		3765		∕	
563	−						

Bunnies

Bow Bunny

Cat and Angel
DMC stranded cotton (floss)

	Xst	BS	FK
326	S	∕	
743	N	∕	▣
781	▓	∕	
801	▓	∕	
909	▓		
912	▣		
945	▤		
954	◢		
957	⊠		
958	▨	∕	
963	←		
964	⊞		
3078	◹		
3716	⊞		
3812	3		

Cat

Angel

Romantic Moments

⬠ Ⓨ ⊥ ⬎ ● ⌄ ◆ + Ⓒ ↑

Stitching is a wonderful way to capture life's romantic moments forever, and the selection of designs in this chapter are suitable for a variety of occasions including weddings, engagements, anniversaries and Valentines Day. The Lover's Glade design captures the scene perfectly; a moment in time when friendship becomes romance and hearts become one forever. And when the happy couple get married the sampler, album cover and ring cushion will make very special keepsakes. Stitched in shades of soft cream, pink and blue, they can be personalised with the name of the bride and groom and the date of the marriage. The romantic cards include a teddy for Valentines Day, a floral card for anniversaries, and a cute cherub for weddings – cards for all the romantic moments in life

Lover's Glade is stitched on antique white Cashel linen, with each stitch worked over two threads of fabric. The chart is on pages 84 and 85.

Lover's Glade

This delightful summer scene with young lovers whispering, swans on the lake, and the glade alive with flowers would make a wonderful engagement or wedding gift

- *Antique White Zweigart Cashel Linen, 28 count 32.5x41cm (13x16in)*
- *DMC stranded cotton (floss) in the colours listed in the key*
- *Tapestry needle, No 24*
- *Picture frame and mount of your choice*

1 Mark the centre of your linen with tacking stitches and oversew around the fabric edges to prevent fraying. Mount the fabric in a frame or embroidery hoop.

2 Work the design from the centre out following the chart and key on pages 84 and 85. Work each stitch over two threads of fabric, using two strands of stranded cotton for the cross stitch, and one strand for the backstitch. Work the foreground before adding the background scene.

Framing the sampler

1 When the design is complete wash and press it following the finishing instructions on page 125. Take your work to a professional framer for mounting and framing, or mount it yourself following the instructions on page 125.

The lake scene in the background of the picture is stitched using one strand of blue stranded cotton (floss).

Mini Wedding Sampler

This mini sampler with embroidered side panels and bead decoration is a perfect wedding or anniversary gift. Names and dates can be added using the alphabet on page 121

- White Zweigart Dublin Linen, 25 count 23x23cm (9x9in)
- DMC stranded cotton (floss) in the colours listed in the key
- DMC rayon thread 30676
- DMC metallic seed bead 08 3046 gold
- DMC seed beads 04 794 blue
- Tapestry needle, No 24
- Picture frame and mount of your choice

1 Mark the centre of your linen with tacking stitches and oversew around the fabric edges. Mount the fabric in an embroidery frame.

2 Work the design from the centre out following the chart and key on pages 86 and 87. The christian names of the bride and groom can be added using the alphabet on page 121. Work each stitch over two threads of fabric, using two strands of stranded cotton for the cross stitch, and one strand for the backstitch. The words 'our wedding' are worked in one strand of rayon thread.

3 The decorative panels at the sides of the sampler are worked using one strand of rayon thread for both the backstitch and the lazy daisy stitches.

4 To work a lazy daisy stitch, bring your thread out through the fabric at the place where you want one end of the stitch to be. Push the needle back through the fabric at this point, then take the needle a short distance along the underside of the fabric. Push the point of the needle out through the fabric where you want the other end of the stitch to be. Wrap the thread over the top of the needle, then bring the needle out through the fabric – you will have made a small oval shaped stitch. Push the needle back into the fabric a short distance away from the top of the stitch to anchor it in place (see diagram on page 125).

5 The beads are attached using one strand of stranded cotton (floss).

The decorative panels down the edges of the sampler are worked in backstitch and lazy daisy stitches using rayon thread with gold seed beads.

Special Moments Album Cover

Make this delightful wedding album cover to match the sampler and the ring cushion. The album can be personalised with the name of the bride and groom

- *White Dublin Linen, 25 count 12.5x28cm (5x11in)*
- *DMC stranded cotton (floss) in the colours listed in the key*
- *DMC rayon thread 30676*
- *DMC metallic seed bead 08 3046 gold*
- *DMC seed beads 04 794 blue*
- *Tapestry needle, No 24*
- *100% cotton needled batting*
- *Mount board, double-sided tape, glue*
- *Wedding album*

1 Mark the centre of your linen with tacking stitches and oversew around the fabric edges. Mount the fabric in an embroidery frame.

2 Work the design from the centre out following the chart and key on pages 86 and 87, and the alphabet on page 121 to add the names. Work each stitch over two threads of fabric, using two strands of

stranded cotton for the cross stitch, and one strand for the backstitch.

3 The word 'wedding' is stitched using two strands of rayon thread. The decorative panel at the bottom of the sampler is stitched using one strand of rayon thread for the backstitch and the lazy daisy stitches (see the wedding sampler on page 77 for details of how to work the lazy daisy stitches). The beads are attached using one strand of stranded cotton.

Making the panel

1 When the design is complete wash and press it following the finishing instructions on page 125.

2 Cut a piece of mount board, slightly larger than the stitched design, but small enough to fit on to the front of the wedding album. Round off the corners of the panel with a sharp knife or scissors. Cut a second panel slightly smaller than the first.

3 Cut a piece of cotton batting slightly smaller than the largest panel. Place the batting on to one side of the panel. Lay the stitching over the top and lace it across the back following the finishing instructions on page 125. Use double-sided tape or glue to attach the smaller piece of mount board to the back of the covered panel. Attach the panel to the front of the wedding album with glue.

Shiny rayon thread has been used to add the lettering and detail stitching to the wedding gifts (see detail photograph).

Ring Cushion

⟨symbols⟩

This pretty ring cushion, with the words 'to love and to cherish' can be used by the bridesmaid or pageboy to carry the wedding rings safely to the altar

- ❧ *White Zweigart Dublin Linen, 25 count 20.5x23cm (8x9in)*
- ❧ *DMC stranded cotton (floss) in the colours listed in the key*
- ❧ *DMC rayon thread 30676*
- ❧ *DMC metallic seed bead 08 3046 gold*
- ❧ *Tapestry needle, No 24*
- ❧ *100% cotton needled batting or white felt, three pieces each 20.5x23cm (8x9in)*
- ❧ *White cotton lace 61cm (24in)*
- ❧ *Gold 2mm ribbon 66cm (26in)*
- ❧ *Gold pins*
- ❧ *shredded paper*

1 Mark the centre of your linen with tacking stitches and oversew around the fabric edges to prevent fraying. Mount the fabric in a frame or embroidery hoop.

2 Work the design from the centre out following the chart and key on pages 86 and 87. Work each stitch over two threads of fabric, using two strands of stranded cotton for the cross stitch, and one strand for the backstitch. The beads are attached using one strand of stranded cotton.

3 When the design is complete wash and press it following the finishing instructions on page 125.

Making the ring cushion

1 Using the template on page 122 as a guide, cut a heart shape from the stitched linen, making sure the stitching is in the centre.

2 Using the same template, cut three heart shapes from cotton batting.

3 With the right side of the stitching facing out, stitch the linen heart to one of the batting hearts with a 6mm (¼in) seam allowance. Stitch the remaining two heart shapes together in the same way to make the bottom of the cushion.

4 Place the lined, stitched heart face down on to the two assembled batting hearts. Pin, then stitch around the outer edge of the heart shapes, with a 1cm (³⁄₈in) seam allowance, and leaving a small gap on one side for turning. Trim away the excess fabric by cutting on the outer stitching line, which will leave a seam allowance of 4mm (⅛in). Clip the edge of the heart by making small cuts in the seam allowance, from the edge of the fabric halfway to the seam.

Stitch the linen heart and the three batting hearts together with a 6mm (¼in) seam allowance (left).
Clip the edge of the heart by making small cuts into the seam allowance, before turning to the right side (right).

5 Turn the heart to the right side through the gap left in the stitching. Cut shredded white paper into short lengths, and use it to stuff the heart. Push the stuffing into the heart using the handle end of a wooden spoon; there should be two layers of batting below the stuffing, and a layer of batting and the stitched design above it. Place the heart on a clean surface and cover with a white cloth. Bang the heart with your fist, until it has a flat top and bottom surface. As you flatten the heart you may have to add more stuffing so that it is hard and tightly packed.

6 Use white sewing thread and small neat stitches to sew up the gap on the edge of the heart.

7 Wrap a length of cotton lace around the outer edge of the heart to cover the seam. Temporarily anchor it in place with pins. Wrap a length of thin gold ribbon around the lace. Thread a gold bead on to a pin, and push it through the ribbon and lace and into the heart. Repeat at regular intervals around the edge of the heart, finishing the ribbon with a bow held in place with a beaded pin.

Beaded pins have been used to secure the lace and the ribbon to the outer edge of the padded ring cushion.

Romantic Occasion Cards

⬜ ⬜ ⬜ ⬜ ⬜ ⬜ ⬜ ⬜ ⬜ ⬜ ⬜

These romantic occasion cards stitched with 'happy wedding day', happy anniversary and 'my Valentine', make wonderful keepsakes of that special day

- 🌸 *White Aida fabric, 14 count 15x10cm (6x4in)*
- 🌸 *DMC stranded cotton (floss) in the colours listed in the key*
- 🌸 *DMC silver metallic thread, colour 5283*
- 🌸 *Tapestry needle, No 24*
- 🌸 *Card with a 10x7cm (4x2³⁄₄in) rectangular aperture for each design*

1 Mark the centre of your Aida fabric with tacking stitches and oversew around the fabric edges to prevent fraying. Mount the fabric in an embroidery hoop.

2 Work the design from the centre out following the chart and key on pages 88 and 89. Use two strands of stranded cotton (floss) for the cross stitch, and one strand for the backstitch and the french knots.

3 The number 25 on the anniversary card is worked using two strands of silver metallic thread for the cross stitch, and one for the backstitch.

4 Wash and press your stitching following the instructions on page 125.

Mounting the stitching in a card

1 Mount the stitching in a ready-made pre-folded card, which has three sections and a window in the middle. Line up your embroidery behind the window opening and then trim the fabric to the correct size and shape to fit the card.

2 Put small lengths of double-sided tape around the window area of the card. Remove the backing from the tape, and lay the card on to the stitching so that the design is lined up correctly in the window. Press firmly in place.

3 Fold the left hand section of the card in to cover the back of the stitching. Ensure the card opens correctly then secure it with double-sided tape.

Use silver metallic thread and the alphabet on page 120 to add numbers to the anniversary card.

Lover's Glade

DMC stranded cotton (floss)

⊡	Blanc	◩	781
◪	307	◸	783
◨	312	◷	839
✷	319	◁	840
▬	320	◺	842
◼	400	◿	910
◿	402	▽	913
◩	433	∧	945
◰	445	H	951
◩	471	⊘	956
↑	472	◉	986
◪	550	+	989
◫	553	✕	3031
→	554	△	3716
◼	600	▷	3755
T	611	◪	3776
S	613	Backstitch	
3	677	╱	319
◼	720	╱	801
N	722	╱	3755
◰	725	French knots	
↓	727	●	433
◖	729	●	3755
÷	775		

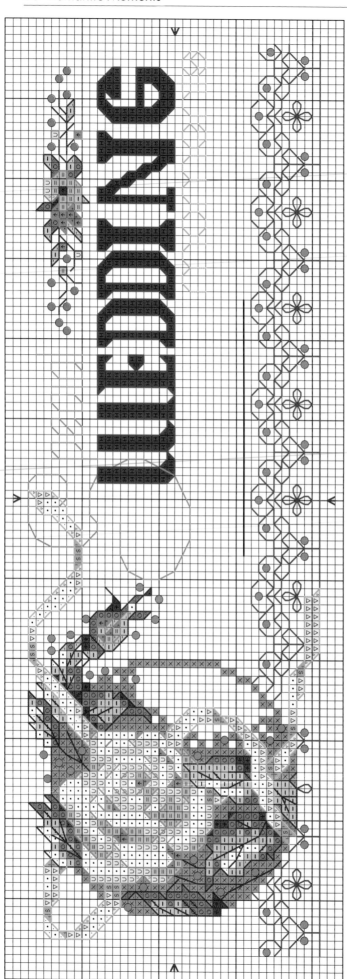

Wedding Keepsakes

DMC stranded cotton (floss)

·	Blanc		Backstitch
←	335	◢	335
◼	435	◢	435
✕	676	◢	729
I	772	◢	3755
▷	775	◢	30676*
∪	818		French knots
‖	3326	●	335
✚	3347	●	30676*
○	3348		Beads
S	3755	◼	3046**
◼	30676*	◼	794**

Lazy daisy stitches

◢	30676*

*DMC Rayon thread **DMC seed beads

Wedding Keepsakes

DMC stranded cotton (floss)

		Backstitch	
⊡	Blanc		
↑	335	⊘	335
→	435	⊘	435
✕	676	⊘	729
−	772	⊘	3755
▽	775	⊘	30676*
Ս	818	French knots	
═	3326	◔	335
✚	3347	●	30676*
⊙	3348	Beads	
S	3755	◉	3046**
H	30676*	◉	794**

Lazy daisy stitches

⊘ 30676*

*DMC Rayon thread
**DMC seed beads

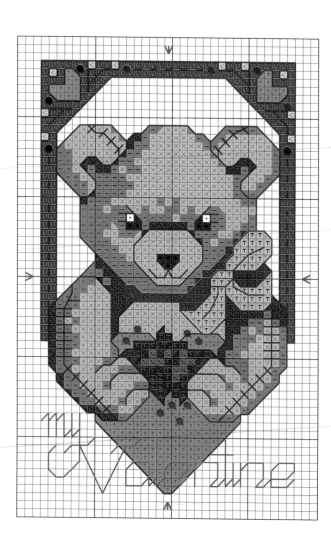

Valentine Card

DMC stranded cotton (floss)

			Backstitch	
·	Blanc			
■	435	⊘	435	
▬	437	⊘	552	
⑨	552	⊘	798	
T	554	⊘	801	
⌂	726	⊘	988	
×	739		French knots	
▽	741	●	434	
⅔	743	◑	726	
◆	801			
<	827			
↑	956			
▨	988			

Wedding Card

DMC stranded cotton (floss)

·	Blanc	▨	3347	
◥	434	▥	3348	
▬	436	⅞	3753	
◪	552		Backstitch	
H	554	⊘	434	
I	720	⊘	552	
<	722	⊘	783	
×	725	⊘	932	
▬	727	⊘	962	
◎	783	⊘	3347	
→	951		French knots	
▽	962	●	434	
S	963			

Anniversary Card

DMC stranded cotton (floss)

⊙	209	◥	✳5283
⊞	211		Backstitch
◼	550	◿	798
⊟	553	◿	801
◣	601	◿	✳5283
H	603		French knots
↑	605	●	798
S	726		
U	905		
▧	907		

✳5283 is DMC metallic silver

Dove Card

DMC stranded cotton (floss)

·	Blanc		Backstitch
◼	304	◿	304
◹	319	◿	319
▨	320	◿	801
◣	413	◿	932
◎	553	◿	3341
⊞	554		French knots
▥	725	●	304
×	738	●	413
◥	799	●	725
▦	801		
S	957		
→	3341		
=	3753		

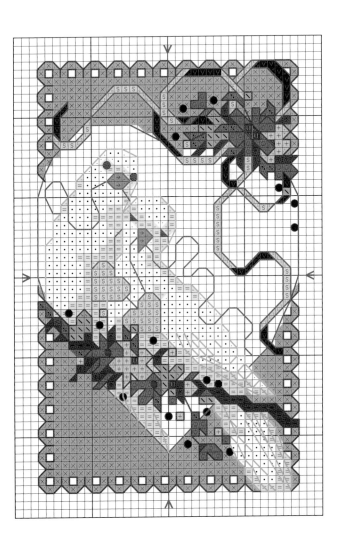

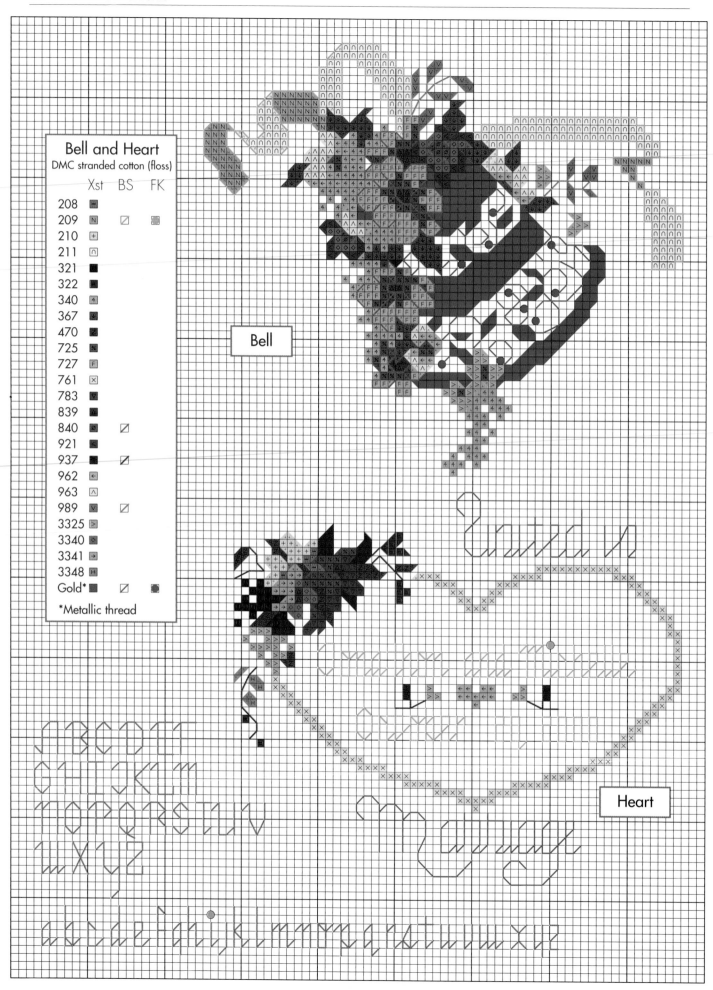

Bell and Heart
DMC stranded cotton (floss)

	Xst	BS	FK
208			
209	N		
210	+		
211	n		
321			
322			
340	+		
367	↓		
470			
725			
727	F		
761	⊠		
783	▼		
839			
840	ø		
921			
937			
962	←		
963	∧		
989	V		
3325	▷		
3340			
3341	→		
3348	H		
Gold*			

*Metallic thread

Bell

Heart

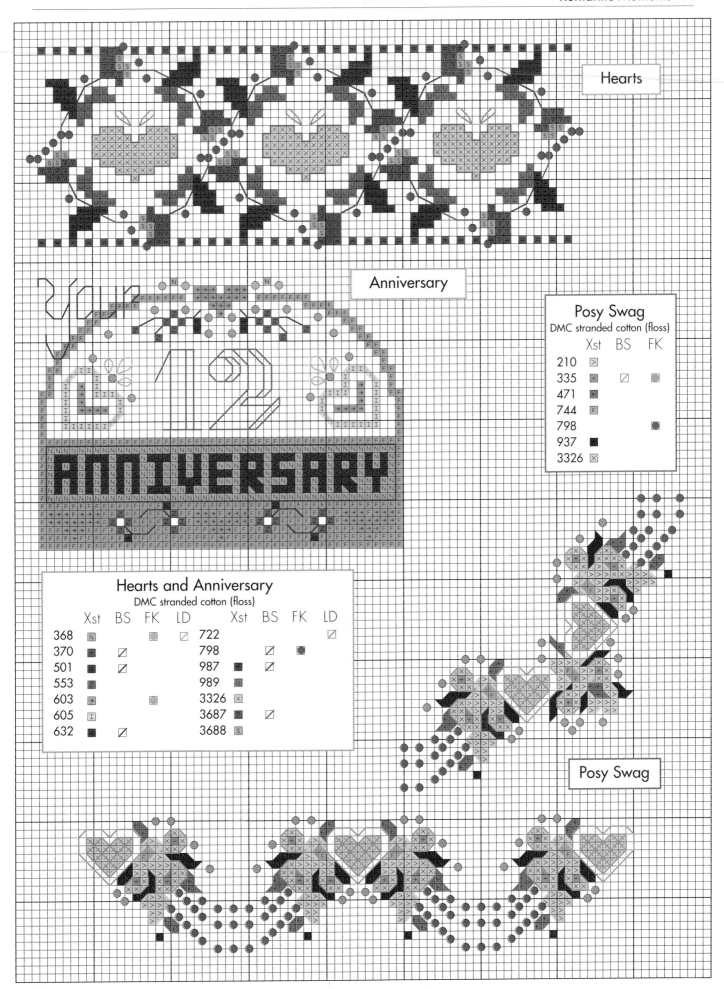

Hearts

Anniversary

Posy Swag
DMC stranded cotton (floss)

	Xst	BS	FK
210	▷		
335	+	◿	◩
471	◪		
744	F		
798			◩
937	■		
3326	⊠		

ANNIVERSARY

Hearts and Anniversary
DMC stranded cotton (floss)

	Xst	BS	FK	LD		Xst	BS	FK	LD
368	N		◩	◿	722				◿
370	◪	◿			798		◿	◉	
501	■	◿			987	+	◿		
553	Z				989	U			
603	→		◩		3326	⊠			
605	I				3687	▽	◿		
632	■	◿			3688	S			

Posy Swag

Tulip

Glory

Tulip, Glory and Rose

DMC stranded cotton (floss)

	Xst	BS	FK
Blanc	·		
309			
322			
326			
741			
818	◎		
839			
841	+	╱	
899	s		
3325	<		
3346			
3347	u		
3348	⊠		

Rose

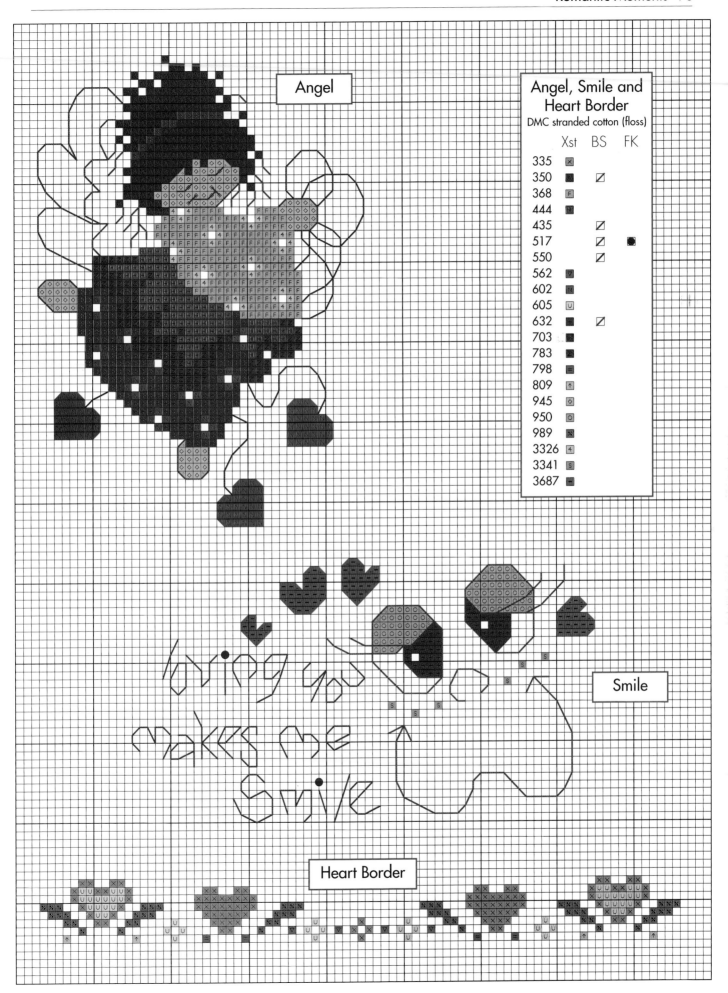

Angel

Smile

Heart Border

Angel, Smile and
Heart Border
DMC stranded cotton (floss)

	Xst	BS	FK
335			
350			
368			
444			
435			
517			
550			
562			
602			
605			
632			
703			
783			
798			
809			
945			
950			
989			
3326			
3341			
3687			

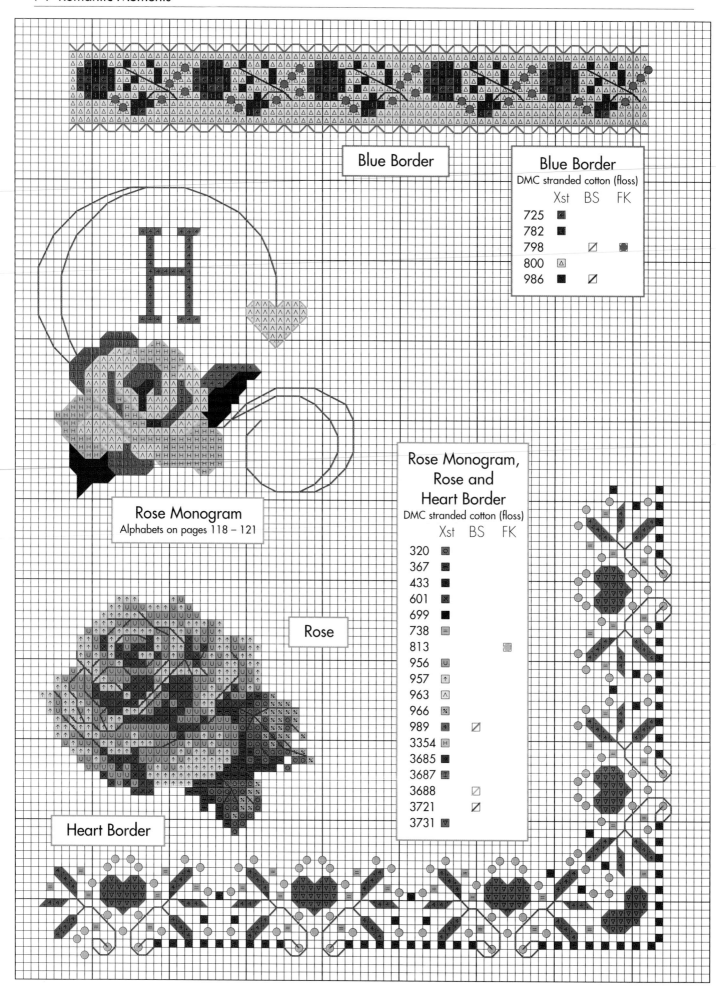

Blue Border

Blue Border
DMC stranded cotton (floss)

	Xst	BS	FK
725	◪		
782	▨		
798		▧	◨
800	△		
986	■	▧	

Rose Monogram
Alphabets on pages 118 – 121

Rose

Rose Monogram, Rose and Heart Border
DMC stranded cotton (floss)

	Xst	BS	FK
320	◉		
367	▦		
433	■		
601	▨		
699	■		
738	▣		
813			▣
956	U		
957	↑		
963	△		
966	▨		
989	▦	▧	
3354	H		
3685	■		
3687	▤		
3688		▧	
3721		▧	
3731	▽		

Heart Border

Bluebird

Bluebird, Love and Butterfly
DMC stranded cotton (floss)

	Xst	BS	FK		Xst	BS	FK
Blanc	·			743			
322				744			
333				745			
335				754			
340	N			776			
352				782			
368				801			
369				813			
402	H			828			
435				840			
603				890			
605				961	S	
722				3716			
725				3776			
741							

Love

Butterfly

Friends are sewn one stitch at a time

Family and Friends

*Family and good friends are some of
the most precious things in life.
In times of joy, and in times of trouble
they are there for you; a friendly
telephone call; much needed
encouragement; a shoulder to cry
on. These are just some of the ways
that friends and family help you in
life. And what nicer way to thank
them than with a hand stitched gift.
The teddy Sampler with teddies of all
shapes, sizes and colours are stitched
around the words 'friends are sewn one
stitch at a time'. The memories
desk set is stitched in soft mauve,
pink and green – the frame can be
used to display a favourite picture;
the address book for keeping in touch,
and the glasses case will show your love
and appreciation for that special
person. The six stitched greetings can
be used in a variety of different ways,
on cards, gift bags, boxes and books*

The nine teddies on this cute teddy sampler are
worked in shades of brown on cream-coloured Aida
fabric. The chart is on pages 106 and 107.

Teddy Bear Sampler

This cute sampler with its stitched message, is a wonderful gift for a friend or for anyone who likes teddies. In place of the message, add a name using one of the alphabets on page 118

- *Cream Aida fabric, 14 count 42.5x35cm (17x14in)*
- *DMC stranded cotton (floss)*
- *Tapestry needle, No 24*
- *Picture frame and mount of your choice*

1 Mark the centre of your Aida fabric with tacking stitches and oversew around the fabric edges to prevent fraying. Mount the fabric in a frame or embroidery hoop.

2 Work the design from the centre out following the chart and key on pages 106 and 107. Use

two strands of stranded cotton for the cross stitch, and one strand for the backstitch and french knots.

Framing the sampler

1 When the design is complete wash and press it following the finishing instructions on page 125. Take your work to a professional framer for mounting and framing, or mount it yourself following the instructions on page 125.

The teddies eyes have been highlighted with french knots using one strand of white stranded cotton (floss). The backstitch message is also stitched using one strand.

Memories Picture Frame

⟨∧⟩ ⟨Y⟩ ⟨⊥⟩ ⟨╲⟩ ⟨●⟩ ⟨╲⟩ ⟨◆⟩ ⟨+⟩ ⟨C⟩ ⟨↑⟩

This pretty floral picture frame is stitched on cream Aida fabric using the chart on page 108, which is assembled on to a frame cut from stiff mounting board

- 🌿 *Cream Aida fabric, 14 count 28x23cm (11x9in)*
- 🌿 *DMC stranded cotton (floss) in the colours listed in the key*
- 🌿 *Tapestry needle, No 24*
- 🌿 *100% cotton batting 18x23cm (7x9in)*
- 🌿 *Mount board – two pieces 18x23cm (7x9in)*
- 🌿 *Self-adhesive picture hanger*
- 🌿 *Double-sided tape, glue*

1 Mark the centre of your Aida fabric with tacking stitches and oversew around the fabric edges to prevent fraying. Mount the fabric in a frame or embroidery hoop.

2 Work the design from the centre out following the chart and key on pages 108 and 109. Use two strands of stranded cotton (floss) for the cross stitch, and one strand for the backstitch and the french knots.

Making the frame

1 Wash and press the stitching following the instructions on page 125. Ask your picture framer to cut two pieces of mount board: one 23x18cm (9x7in) with a 12.5x10cm (5x4in) hole cut in the centre, and the other slightly smaller than 23x18cm (9x7in) to use for the back.

2 Cut a piece of cotton batting slightly smaller then the mount board cut for the frame front. Glue the batting on to the board. Temporarily attach the stitching to the batting on the mount board using strips of double-sided tape. Make sure that the hole cut in the board is exactly in the centre of the stitching.

Following the diagram above, and with the stitching held up to a light or the window, cut away the central Aida panel, leaving approximately 1.25cm (½in) of fabric for turning to the reverse side. Cut away the Aida around the outside edges of board, again leaving 1.25cm (½in) for turning on to the back. Remove the Aida from the batting, and peel away the double-sided tape.

3 Lay the stitching face down on a flat surface, on top of this place the front board, batting side down. Fold the excess fabric at the edges of the board over and glue them to the reverse side of the board.

4 With the stitched side facing you, and holding the covered board up to a window, make cuts in the Aida fabric into the four corners of the central panel.

5 Wrap the excess fabric over, and glue it to the back of the board.

6 Place a photograph behind the opening in the frame, and then glue the back board in place. Attach a self-adhesive hanger to the back of the frame.

Floral Glasses Case

This useful glasses case is made from plain cotton fabric, which is padded and then machine quilted to give the glasses extra protection

A large wooden button has been used to decorate the flap on the quilted glasses case.

- *Cream Aida fabric, 18 count 12.5x11.5cm (5x4½in)*
- *DMC stranded cotton (floss) in the colours listed in the key*
- *Tapestry needle, No 24*
- *100% cotton batting, 34x11cm (13½x4¼in)*
- *Cotton fabric – two pieces 34x11cm (13½x4¼)*
- *Seam binding 6mm (¼in) – 30cm (12in)*
- *Button*
- *Velcro spot fastener*
- *Sewing thread and needle*

1 Mark the centre of your Aida fabric with tacking stitches and oversew around the fabric edges to prevent fraying. Mount the fabric in a frame or embroidery hoop.

2 Work the design from the centre out following the chart and key on page 109. Use two strands of stranded cotton (floss) for the cross stitch, and one strand for the backstitch and french knots, apart from the lettering which is done in two strands.

3 Wash and press your stitching following the instructions on page 125.

Making the glasses case

1 To make the top flap, cut the Aida fabric to size using the template on page 122 – 11cm (4¼in)

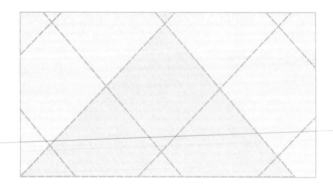

Use a sewing machine to make a grid of stitched lines every 4.5cm (1¾in) across the fabric.

high x 9cm (3⅝in) wide. Round off the bottom corners of the Aida.

2 Sew seam binding down both sides and along the bottom edge of the shaped Aida.

3 Sandwich the cotton batting between the two layers of cotton fabric. Pin and then tack the layers together. Use a sewing machine to make a grid of stitched lines every 4.5cm (1¾in) across the fabric.

4 Pin the stitched Aida, right side facing the quilted fabric on to one short edge. Sew, then neaten the seam. Turn over, then stitch the other short edge of the quilted fabric. Fold the quilted fabric in half, so that the Aida flap is inside the bag, and the short edges come together. Pin, then stitch the two long edges of the bag. Neaten the seams then turn the bag to the right side.

5 Sew a velcro spot on to the underside of the Aida flap and also on to the quilted bag to hold the flap shut. Sew a button on the outer flap to correspond with the velcro spot.

Floral Address Book

Use the alphabet on page 121 to personalise this useful address book with a single initial. The design is also the right shape and size to be mounted into a small oval greetings card

- *Cream Aida fabric, 14 count 12.5x9cm (5x3½in)*
- *DMC stranded cotton (floss) in the colours listed in the key*
- *Tapestry needle, No 24*
- *Address book with a 9x5.5cm (3½x 2¼in) oval aperture*

1 Mark the centre of your Aida fabric with tacking stitches and oversew around the fabric edges to prevent fraying. Mount the fabric in an embroidery hoop.

2 Work the design from the centre out following the chart and key on page 109. Use three strands of

stranded cotton (floss) for the cross stitch, and one strand for the backstitch and french knots. Use the alphabet on page 121 to add an initial to the design.

3 Wash and press your stitching following the instructions on page 125.

Making the address book

1 The address book has a three-folded card attached to the top, and the stitching should be mounted using the card instructions on page 82.

The address book is stitched on cream Aida fabric in soft shades of mauve, pink and green. An initial can be added using the alphabet on page 121.

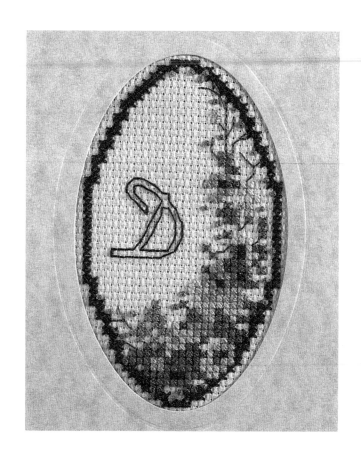

Stitched Greetings

These quick-to-stitch designs can be used in greetings cards, or to decorate a gift bag, notebook, box or small cushion

- *Cream Aida fabric, 14 count 11.5x11.5cm (4½x4½in) for each design*
- *DMC stranded cotton (floss) in the colours listed in the key*
- *Tapestry needle, No 24*
- *Mount board*
- *Wadding*
- *Length of upholstery cord*
- *Gingham fabric, two pieces 18x18cm (7x7in)*
- *DMC perle cotton, pink*
- *White sewing thread and needle*
- *Small buttons*

1 Mark the centre of your Aida fabric with tacking stitches and oversew around the fabric edges to prevent fraying. Mount the fabric in an embroidery hoop.

2 Work the design from the centre out following the chart and key on pages 110 and 111. Use two strands of stranded cotton (floss) for the cross stitch, and one strand for the backstitch, french knots, and lazy daisy stitch (see page 124 for stitch instructions), apart from the backstitch on the Dad design which is worked in two strands.

3 Wash and press your stitching following the instructions on page 125.

4 Fray the edges of the fabric before attaching it to the front of a card, gift bag, or book.

Assembling the box top

1 To mount the design on the top of a gift box. Cut a piece of board just smaller than the top of a box. Lace the design on to the board, padding it with wadding. Glue the mounted design on to the top of the box. Glue the upholstery cord around the edges of the design.

3 Attach the stitching to the gingham fabric with blanket stitches (see page 124), worked around the edges of the Aida using perle cotton.

4 Use the perle cotton to work a row of large running stitches around the outer edges of the cushion. Sew buttons, one on to each of the four corners of the design.

Assembling the cushion

1 The cushion is made by sewing the two squares of gingham fabric together around the outer edges, leaving a small gap for turning. Turn the cushion through the gap to the right side. Stuff lightly with wadding, and sew up the gap.

2 Cut the stitched Aida down to a 9cm (3½in) square. Turn the edges 6mm (¼in) over on to the wrong side of the fabric. Pin then tack the design on to the middle of one side of the cushion.

The photograph opposite shows how the six stitched greetings can be made into cards, gift bags, a box, book and cushion.

Teddy Sampler

DMC stranded cotton (floss)

⊡	Blanc	◸	840
■	301	↑	842
+	402	✕	932
■	433	Z	950
■	434	✳	3345
↓	435	◹	3347
I	436	F	3348
=	437	■	3371
S	543	✸	3781
→	676	N	3782
⊠	677	**Backstitch**	
■	680	◹	720
◈	702	◹	725
▽	704	◹	931
▥	720	◹	3345
H	722	◹	3371
◂	725	◹	3781
◉	727	**French knots**	
◺	738	◖	Blanc
✓	739	▨	727
■	801		

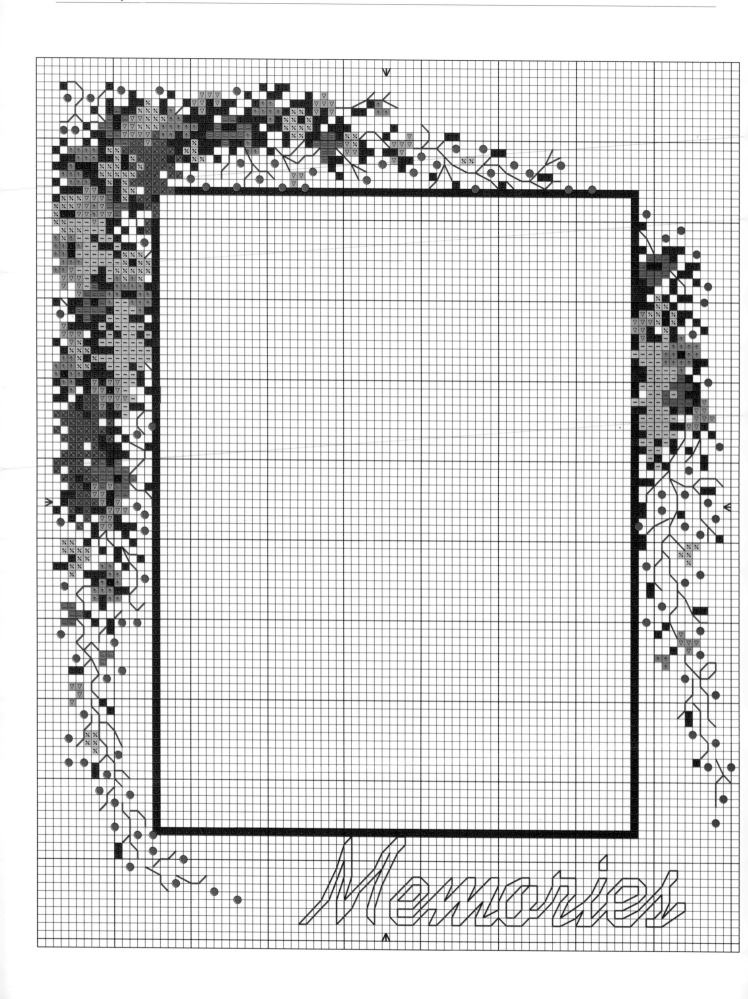

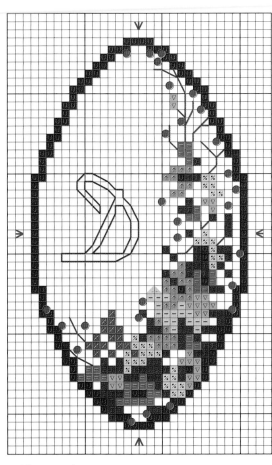

Address Book

Memories Desk Set

DMC stranded cotton (floss)

☒	208		Backstitch
−	210	⧄	433
Ц	433	⧄	987
⁒	605	⧄	3731
⊟	722		French knots
↑	744	⬤	208
▽	813		
■	987		
⬚	3731		

Glasses Case

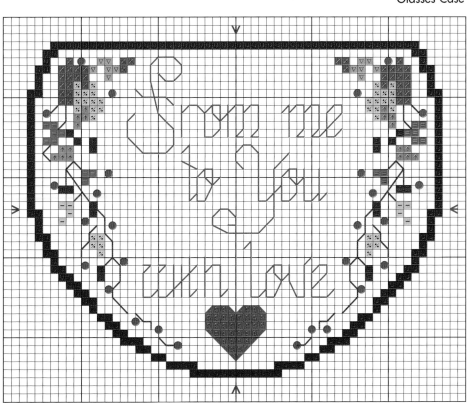

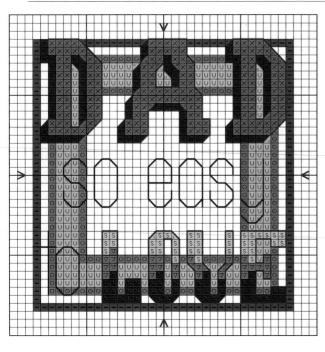

Dad

DMC stranded cotton (floss)

■	312	**Backstitch**	
◯	334	⧄	829
■	829	⧄	3362
Ⴎ	3325	⧄	3777
■	3362		
✕	3364		
■	3777		
▽	3778		
S	3779		

Mom

DMC stranded cotton (floss)

+	209	⧄	402
↑	402	⧄	435
▬	435	⧄	604
◯	604	⧄	727
Ⴎ	727	⧄	801
■	801	⧄	989
S	986	**French knots**	
Backstitch		◉	604
⧄	209	◉	801

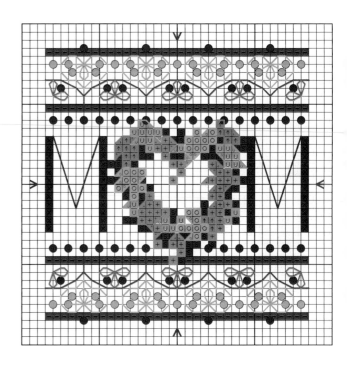

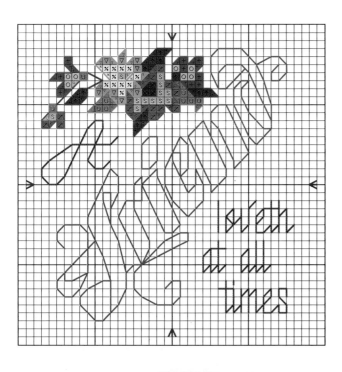

Friends

DMC stranded cotton (floss)

▽	209	**Backstitch**	
⁒	211	⧄	209
■	300	⧄	300
Z	725	⧄	718
S	727	⧄	725
▨	987	⧄	987
Ⴎ	989	⧄	989
+	3760	⧄	3760
◯	3766		

Teddy Friends

DMC stranded cotton (floss)

■	433		Backstitch
■	434	☑	792
⬆	436	☑	938
✕	738		French knots
◉	801	●	792
■	938		
✕	3716		

Work of Heart

DMC stranded cotton (floss)

I	208	⬆	3348	☑	3348
Z	210	✕	3354	☑	3731
H	211		Backstitch		French knots
◉	726	☑	208	●	3731
✕	797	☑	434		
▽	799	☑	726		
S	800	☑	797		
■	3345	☑	3345		
U	3347	☑	3347		

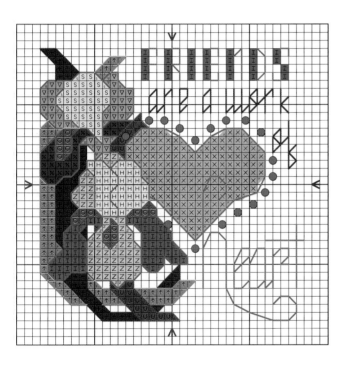

Family

DMC stranded cotton (floss)

■	310		Backstitch		French knots
◉	726	☑	310	●	310
–	776	☑	335	●	550
■	839	☑	550	●	988
▨	973	☑	839		
U	986	☑	986		
⬆	988	☑	988		
✕	3756	☑	3325		
✕	3820				

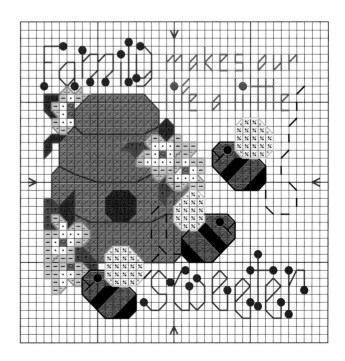

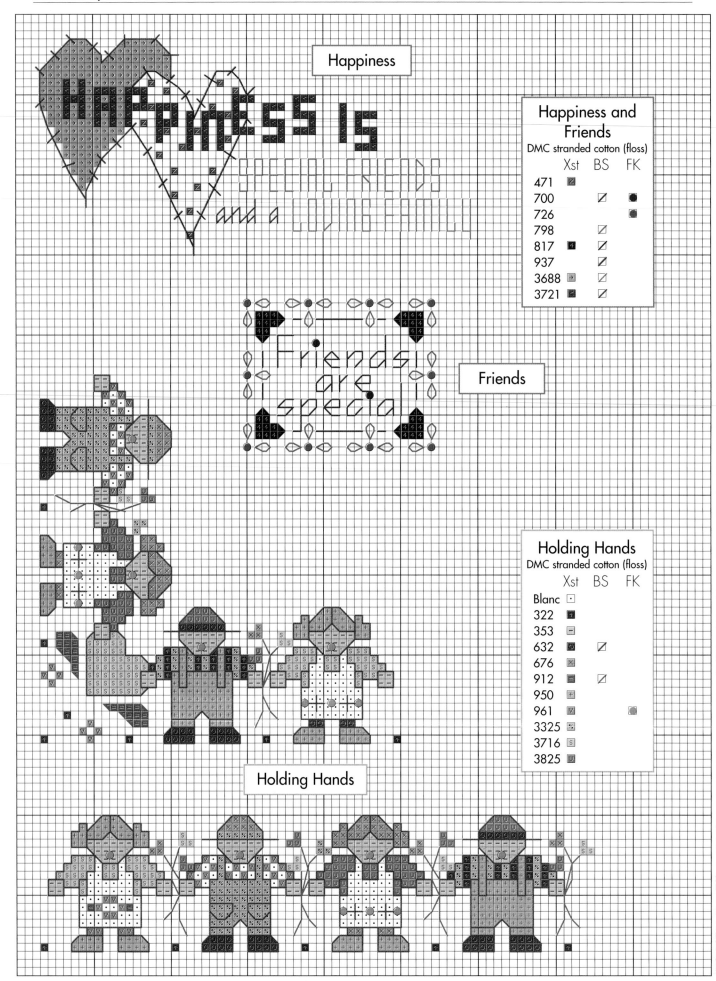

Happiness

Friends

Holding Hands

Happiness and Friends
DMC stranded cotton (floss)

	Xst	BS	FK
471	▨		
700		▨	●
726			●
798		▨	
817	◪	▨	
937		▨	
3688	▨	▨	
3721	▨	▨	

Holding Hands
DMC stranded cotton (floss)

	Xst	BS	FK
Blanc	⊡		
322	◼		
353	▭		
632	◉	▨	
676	▨		
912	▨	▨	
950	＋		
961	▽		◼
3325	▨		
3716	S		
3825	◰		

Mom/Dad

Mom/Dad and Mom Heart
DMC stranded cotton (floss)

	Xst	BS	FK		Xst	BS	FK
209		☑		907	▣	☑	
211	Σ			956	Z		▦
322		☑	▣	957	F		
518	⊞		▣	3325	H		
519	✕			3354	N		
562	▽	☑		3347	▦		
632	▩	☑		3348	▥		
725			◉	3731	▦	☑	
904	▪	☑		3790		☑	
906	▩						

Life Sampler
DMC stranded cotton (floss)

	Xst	BS	FK		Xst	BS	FK
322	▣			986	▪	☑	◉
326	▤		◉	989	▨	☑	
899	↑			3822	U		▣
931		☑	◉				

Mom

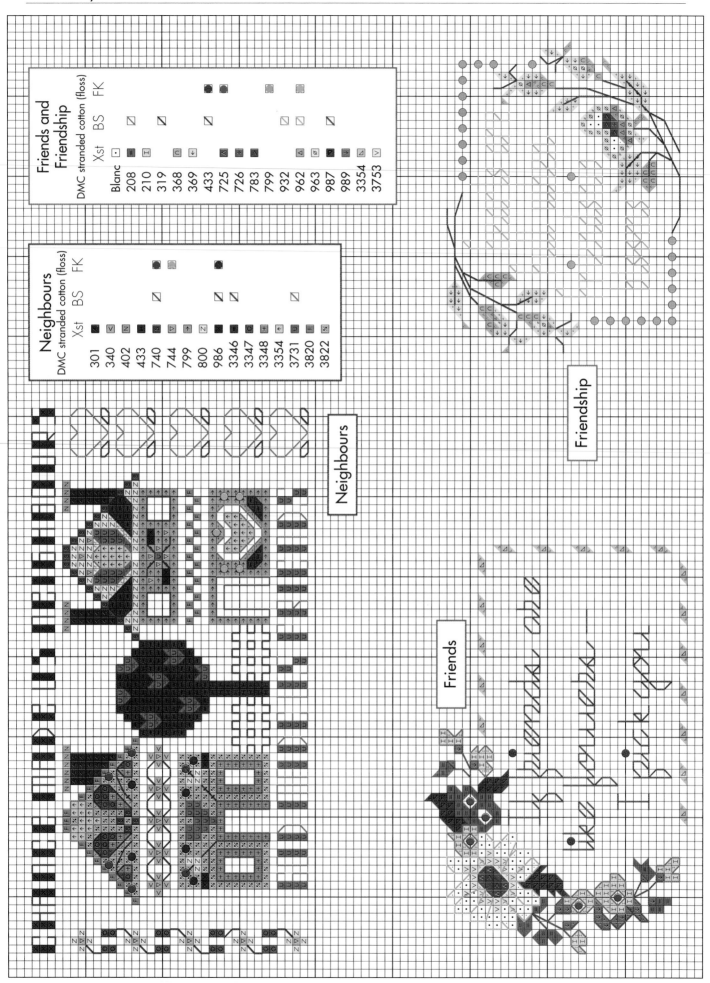

Friends and Friendship

DMC stranded cotton (floss)

	Xst	BS	FK
Blanc	·		
208			
210	H		
319			
368	C		
369	↓		
433	◄		
725	↗		
726	◣		
783	◄		
799	◩		
932	⌀		
962	◼		
963	◿		
987	∇		
989			
3354			
3753			

Neighbours

DMC stranded cotton (floss)

	Xst	BS	FK
301	◼		
340	V		
402	N		
433	⊞		
740	S		
744	▷		
799	↑		
800	N		
986			
3346	◼		
3347	⊘		
3348	+		
3354	←		
3731	⊔		
3820	⊟		
3822	⊠		

Neighbours

Friendship

Friends

Grandpa

Grandpa and Dad
DMC stranded cotton (floss)

	Xst	BS	FK
367	■		
433	■	◪	
434	■		
436	→		
437	z		
469		◪	
801	■		
890		◪	
938		◪	
3371		◪	

Dad

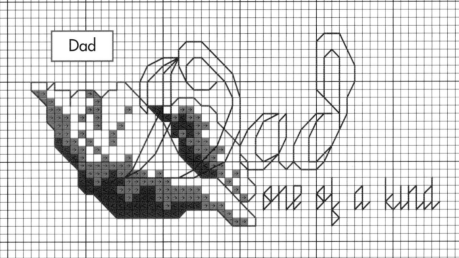

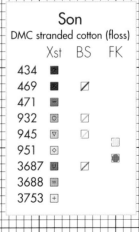

Son
DMC stranded cotton (floss)

	Xst	BS	FK
434	■		
469	■	◪	
471	▬		
932	◎	◪	
945	▽	◪	
951	◇		●
3687	⊎	◪	
3688	▤		
3753	⊞		

Son

Brother

Patchwork

Bird

Bird

Brother and Patchwork
DMC stranded cotton (floss)

	Xst	BS	FK		Xst	BS	FK
210				798			
221				813			
224				828			
310				839			
321				841			
434				986			
721				3047			
722				3345			
725				3350			
727				3722			
754				3733			

Bird
DMC stranded cotton (floss)

	Xst	BS	FK
Blanc			
307			
310			
319			
718			
775			
3341			
3347			
3348			
3713			
3746			
3770			
3755			

when friends are together

HEARTS SPEAK
WITHOUT WORDS

Hearts

Sister

I ♥ You
Sister

LOVE AT FIRST
if you don't
SUCCEED
ask Grandma

Grandma

	Hearts, Sister and Grandma DMC stranded cotton (floss)		
	Xst	BS	FK
Blanc	⊡		
210	⊠		
224	◄		
310	■	◪	
402	▽		
415	S		
552		◪	
676	◁		
700	▣		
726	▣		
729	▣	◪	▣
780	▣	◪	
782	⊠		
799	↑		
958		◪	
959	÷		
3346	▩	◪	
3687	✛	◪	
3689	U		
3760		◪	▣
3816	○	◪	
3818	▣	◪	

Alphabet Library

Use the alphabets on the next four pages to personalise the projects in this book. A page reference for where each alphabet has been used is indicated on the charts

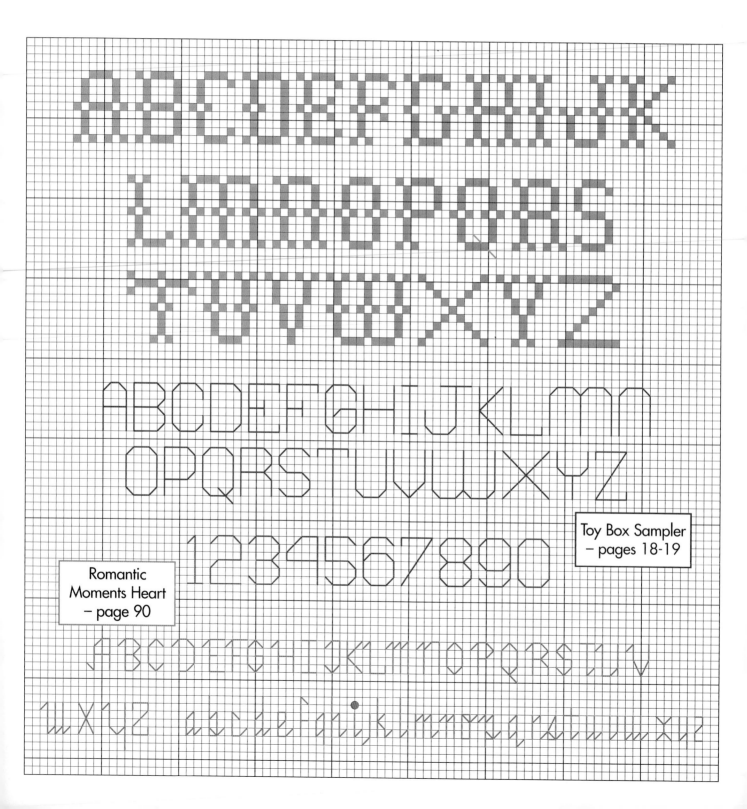

Toy Box Sampler
– pages 18-19

Romantic
Moments Heart
– page 90

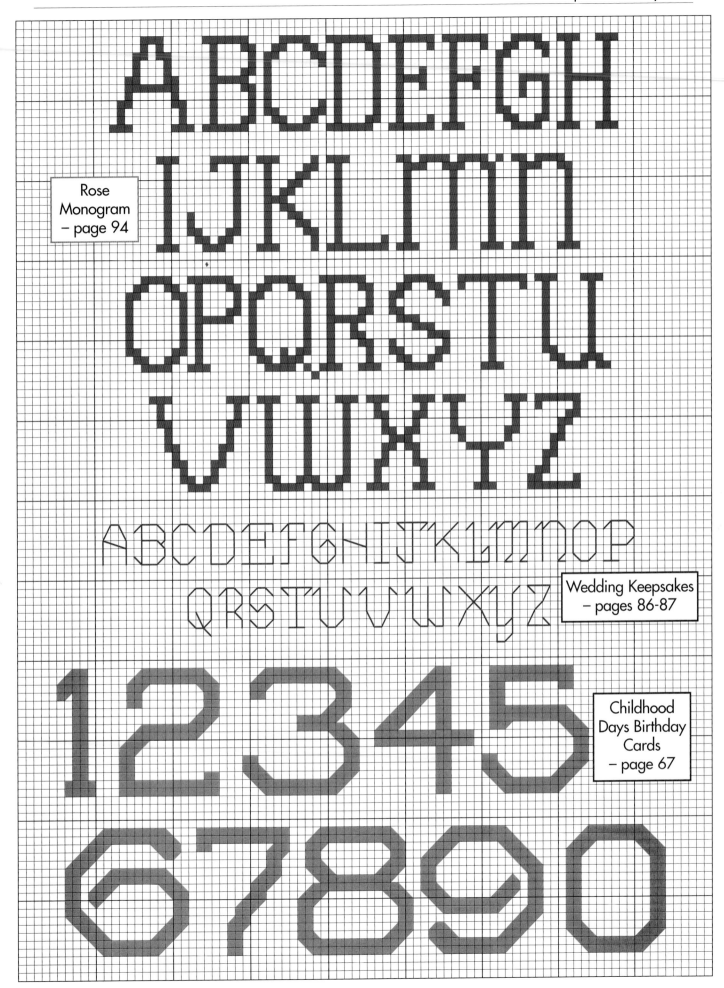

Rose
Monogram
– page 94

Wedding Keepsakes
– pages 86-87

Childhood
Days Birthday
Cards
– page 67

Childhood Days
– page 64

Anniversary Card
– page 89
Anniversary – page 91

ABCDEFGHIJ
KLMNOPQR
STUVWXYZ

Fairy-Tale Sampler
– pages 62-63

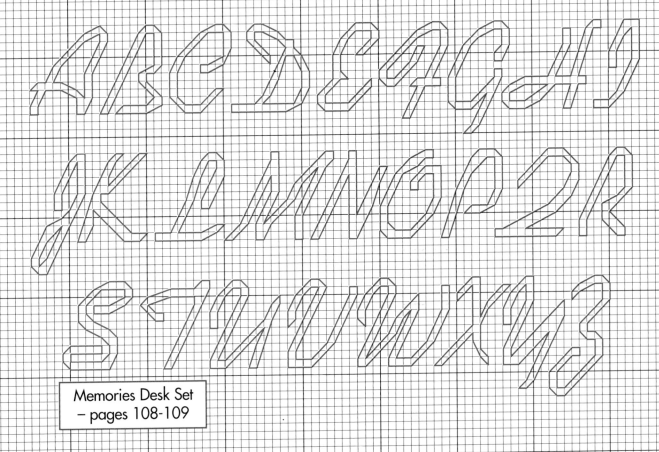

Memories Desk Set
– pages 108-109

ABCDEFGHIJKLMNOPQRSTUVWXYZ 1234567890

Wedding Keepsakes – pages 86-87

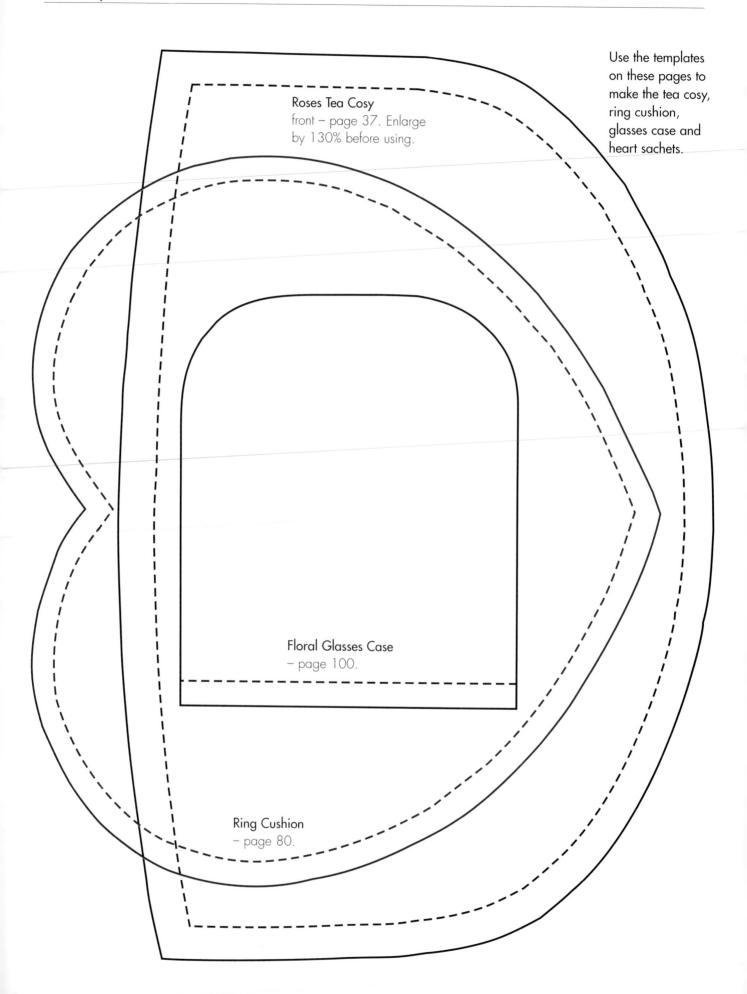

Roses Tea Cosy
front – page 37. Enlarge
by 130% before using.

Use the templates
on these pages to
make the tea cosy,
ring cushion,
glasses case and
heart sachets.

Floral Glasses Case
– page 100.

Ring Cushion
– page 80.

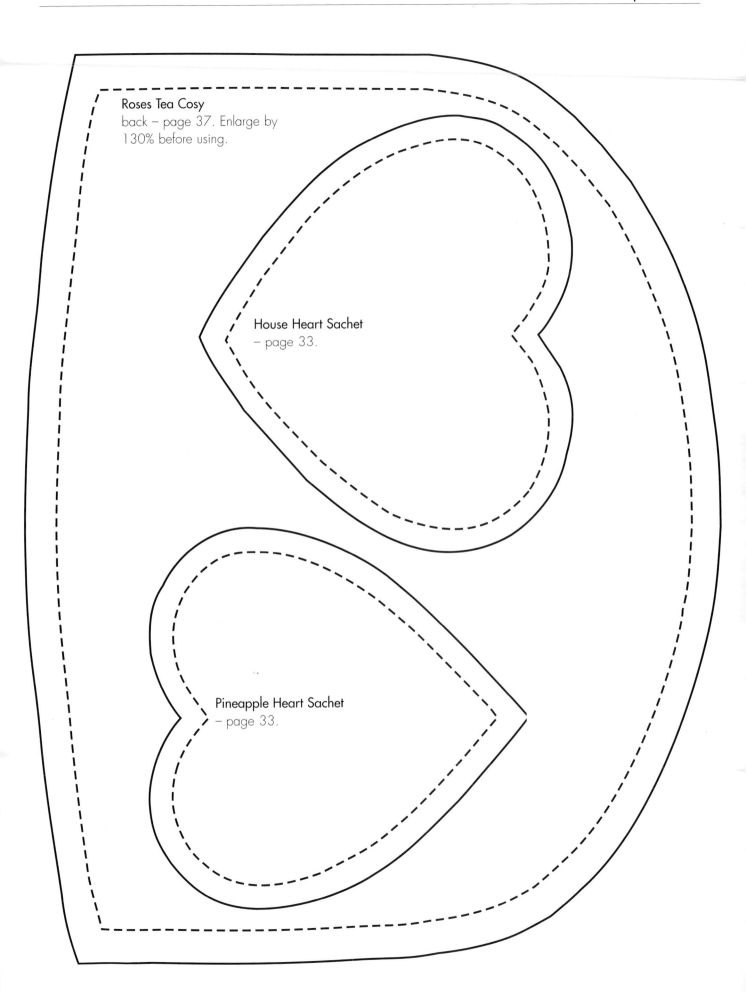

Roses Tea Cosy
back – page 37. Enlarge by
130% before using.

House Heart Sachet
– page 33.

Pineapple Heart Sachet
– page 33.

Essential Techniques

Starting and Finishing

To start off your first length of thread, make a knot at one end and push the needle through to the back of the fabric, about 3cm (1¼in) from your starting point, leaving the knot on the right side. Stitch towards the knot, securing the thread at the back of the fabric as you go. When the thread is secure, cut off the knot.

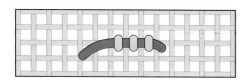

To finish off a thread or start new threads, simply weave the thread into the back of several worked stitches and then trim off neatly.

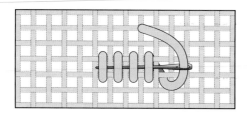

Cross Stitch

Each coloured square on the chart represents one cross on the evenweave fabric. If the fabric is linen each stitch would be worked over two threads of fabric. A cross stitch is worked in two stages: a diagonal stitch is worked over one block of fabric (Aida), or two threads (finer fabric like linen) from the bottom left of the stitch to the top right. The second part of the stitch is worked in the opposite direction to form a cross.

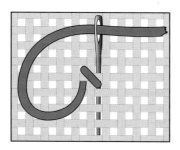

Backstitch and Outlining

Backstitch is indicated on the charts by a solid coloured line. It is worked on its own, on top of stitches for detail, or as an outline around areas of cross stitch to give definition.

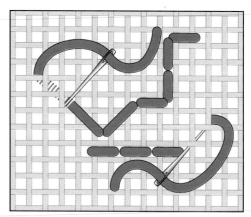

Blanket Stitch

This stitch is used to edge fabric to stop it fraying and for decoration. Bring the needle out on the lower line shown in the diagram below. Re-insert the needle at 1 on the upper line and out again at 2, keeping the thread under the needle point so a loop is formed.

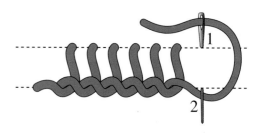

Lazy Daisy Stitch

Bring your needle and thread out through the fabric, then push just the point of the needle back into the fabric at the same place. Take the needle a short distance along the back of the fabric, then push it out where you want the other end of the stitch to be. Wrap the thread over the top of the needle, then pull the needle out of the fabric. You will have made a small oval stitch. Make a small stitch at the top of the oval to anchor it in place.

Quilting Stitch

To quilt the fabric layers together, make a row of small neat running stitches through all the layers of fabric, passing the thread under and over the fabric with regular spacing.

Attaching Beads on the Cross

Use two strands of stranded cotton (floss) to attach a bead on to the top of a cross stitch. Thread the bead on to the needle as you make the first part of the cross, then as you make the second part of the cross lay one thread of stranded cotton (floss) either side of the bead, before pushing the needle back into the fabric and continuing with the stitching.

Washing and Ironing Cross Stitch

Handling even the smallest piece of cross stitch can make the threads look flat and dull, so always wash your work before it is framed or mounted. Swish your stitching in luke warm water and, if the colours bleed, rinse with fresh water until the water is clear. Do not be tempted to stop rinsing unless you are absolutely sure the bleeding has stopped. Roll your stitching up in a clean towel and squeeze gently to remove most of the water. On a second, fluffy towel, place your design face down, cover with a clean cloth and iron until the stitching is dry.

Mounting and Framing

It is best to take large cross stitch designs to a professional framer who will advise you on displaying your work. If you would prefer to lace your own work then most framers will be happy to make the frame and cut the mount and backboard for you. If you are mounting the work yourself use acid-free board in a pale colour. The mount board should be cut to fit inside your picture frame, allowing for the thickness of material that will be wrapped over the board. There are two methods of attached the stitching to the board – taping and lacing.

Taping

Place the cut board on the reverse side of your stitching. Starting from the centre of one of the longest sides, fold the excess fabric over on to the board, then pin through the fabric and into the edge of the board. Repeat along all four sides of the board. Use strips of double-sided tape to hold the fabric on to the back of the board. Remove the pins once the work is secured.

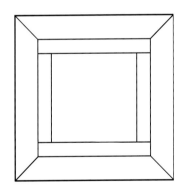

Lacing

Pin the work along the edges of the board in the same way as for the taping. Working from the centre of one side, and using very long lengths of strong thread begin lacing backwards and forwards across the gap between the fabric overlap, while keeping the fabric on the right side stretched. Remove the pins. Repeat for the other two sides, taking care to mitre the corners or turn the corners in neatly.

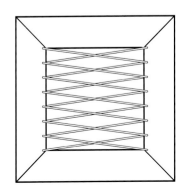

Acknowledgements

The publishers would like to thank the following people:
Jo Strowger, Barbara Phillips, Christine Thompson, Michaela Learner, Yvonne Tudgay,
Doreen Holland and Sue Gully for their expert stitching;
John Gollop for his excellent photography; and Susan and Martin Penny for editing and
designing the book, and preparing the charts.

Suppliers

When writing to any of the companies listed below, please include a stamped addressed
envelope for your reply.

Framecraft
372-376 Summer Lane, Hockley, Birmingham,
B19 3QA
*Mill Hill beads, perforated paper, Sudberry carriage
clock and key rings.*

DMC Creative World Ltd
Pullman Road, Wigston, Leicester LE8 2DY
*Zweigart Aida and linen, stranded cotton and baby
bootees.*

Coats Crafts Ltd
PO Box 22, The Lingfield Estate, McMullen Road,
Darlington, Co Durham DL1 1YQ
Balger blending filament and hooded baby towel.

Craft Creations Ltd
2C Ingersoll House, Dalamare Road, Cheshunt,
Herts EN8 9ND
Greetings card blanks.

The DMC Corporation
Port Kearney Bld, 10 South Kearney,
NJ 070732-0650, USA
Zweigart Aida, linen and stranded cotton.

Gay Bowles Sales Inc
PO Box 1060, Janesville, WI, USA

Anne Brinkley Designs Inc
761 Palmer Avenue, Holmdel, NJ 97733, USA

Ireland Needlecraft Pty Ltd
2-4 Keppel Drive, Hallam, Victoria 3803, Australia

DMC Needlecraft Pty
PO Box 317, Earlswood 2206, New South Wales
2204, Australia
Zweigart Aida, linen and stranded cotton.

Chart Subject Index

Index

⟨symbols⟩

Entries in *italics* indicate illustrations,
bold indicates charts.